marriage
IS ORDAINED OF GOD
BUT

WHO CAME UP WITH
dating?

marriage

IS ORDAINED OF GOD

BUT

WHO CAME UP WITH

dating?

CHAS HATHAWAY

CFI
Springville, Utah

ISBN 13: 978-1-59955-904-9

Published by CFI an imprint of Cedar Fort, Inc., 2373 W. 700 S., Springville, UT 84663
Distributed by Cedar Fort, Inc. www.cedarfort.com

LIBRARY OF CONGRESS CATALOGING-IN-PUBLICATION DATA

Hathaway, Chas, 1979- , author.
  Marriage is ordained of God, but who came up with dating? / Chas Hathaway.
    p. cm.
  Summary: A dating guide for LDS singles ages 14 to 30 that uses quotes
from latter-day prophets and personal experiences of the author.
  ISBN 978-1-59955-904-9
  1. Dating (Social customs) 2. Dating (Social customs)--Religious
aspects--Church of Jesus Christ of Latter-day Saints. 3. Marriage. 4.
Marriage--Religious aspects--Church of Jesus Christ of Latter-day Saints.
I. Title.

  HQ801.H357 2011
  241'.6765088289332--dc22

  2011012178

Cover design by Angela D. Olsen
Cover design © 2011 by Lyle Mortimer
Edited and typeset by Melissa J. Caldwell

Printed in the United States of America

10 9 8 7 6 5 4 3 2 1

Printed on acid-free paper

For the girl who gave me a chance.
I love you, Jenni!

contents

Introduction:
The Most
Important Decision

In researching for this book, Jenni and I have discovered a principle that has been repeated over and over and over by the leaders of the Church. It has been repeated by prophets and apostles since the beginning of this dispensation. In fact, this principle is almost always quoted using phrases like, "the *most* important," or "the *greatest*," which, coming from a prophet, ought to get our attention.

Want to know what it is?

Too bad. You'll have to find it yourself.

Just kidding. The repeated principle we have come across is that the most important decision you will make in your life is *who you will marry.*

Wow! That's quite a statement, isn't it? The *most important* decision you will make is who you will marry. What about the decision to get baptized? What about the decision to go on a mission or to have children? Those are pretty important, aren't they? Why would the decision of *who* to marry be the most important decision of your whole life?

Maybe we can gather some insight from reading some of these statements by the prophets:

Bruce R. McConkie was speaking to BYU students when he said:

I believe that the most important single thing that any Latter-day Saint ever does in this world is to marry the right person, in the right place, by the right authority; and that then—when they have been so sealed by the power and authority which Elijah the prophet restored—the most important remaining thing that any Latter-day Saint can ever do is so to live that the terms and conditions of the covenant thus made will be binding and efficacious now and forever.[1]

Gordon B. Hinckley shared the same doctrine in a priesthood conference when he said:

I could wish for you nothing more wonderful than the love, the absolute total love, of a companion of whom you are proud and worthy in every respect. This choice will be the most important of all the choices you make in your life. I pray that heaven may smile upon you in the choice you make, that you may be guided, that you may live without regret.[2]

In another instance, President Hinckley said it this way:

Every normal young man desires a wife. Every normal young woman desires a husband. Be worthy of the mate you choose. Respect him or her. Give encouragement to him or her. Love your companion with all your heart. This will be the most important decision of your life, the individual whom you marry.

There is no substitute for marrying in the temple. It is the only place under the heavens where marriage can be solemnized for eternity. Don't cheat yourself. Don't cheat your companion. Don't shortchange your lives. Marry the right person in the right place at the right time.[3]

President Thomas S. Monson, speaking of meeting his wife and deciding that she was the girl he wanted to pursue, said, "That decision, I believe, was perhaps the most important that I have ever made."[4] He then quoted both President Hinckley and Bruce R. McConkie in the quotes above.

After hearing these statements, some might ask, "If this is the most important decision I will ever make, then why are there so many rules about when I can date and how I can date? Why must I be morally clean?"

I think the answer is found in the prophets' statements. They didn't say that the most important decision you will ever make is that you get married—they said the most important decision is who you will marry, where you marry, and by what authority. The focus is not on the act itself, but on the person, on the quality, and the potential of the relationship. If you simply get married just to get married, then you have completely missed the point. If you plan to marry just because you are in love, or because the two of you have so much in common, or because you communicate well, then you have not been listening closely to the prophets. And by the same token, if you decide that marriage isn't for you, that it's not your "thing," then maybe you ought to listen more carefully.

I suppose one of the reasons there is so much focus on morality and high standards in dating is because by living those principles, you best align yourself to both find and become the right person. Neglecting those standards burns the bridge to a happy, successful marriage. If you have already burned that bridge, rebuilding it through sincere repentance is painful, challenging, and time consuming. Yet it is also well worth it—but we will discuss that later.

So how should you approach marriage? How do you know who to marry? Well, that's the intent of this book. To help you become the right person so you can find the right person at the right time, so you can marry in the right place and have a loving, happy, marriage.

NOTES

1. Bruce R. McConkie, "Agency or Inspiration—Which?" in *Brigham Young University 1972–73 Speeches*, 27 Feb. 1973.
2. Gordon B. Hinckley, "Living Worthy of the Girl You Will Someday Marry," *Ensign*, May 1998, 49.
3. Gordon B. Hinckley, "Life's Obligations," *Ensign*, Feb. 1999, 2.
4. Thomas S. Monson, "Life's Greatest Decisions," CES Fireside for Young Adults, 7 Sept. 2003.

Pre-Sixteen

Rejoice, O young man, in thy youth; and let thy
heart cheer thee in the days of thy youth, and walk
in the ways of thine heart, and in the sight of thine
eyes: but know thou, that for all these things God
will bring thee into judgment.
—Ecclesiastes 11:9

one

First Dance

The first dance I ever attended was in the fifth grade, but I made sure not to dance with anyone. I even came up with a strategy to avoid dancing on the girls-choice dances, since I never would have asked anyone myself. Wallflowers usually ended up dancing with someone at some point, so as soon as the music started, I would walk around the middle of the dance floor as if headed somewhere.

Sometimes I would dance in place for a moment if a teacher was near. Teachers were good at setting people up. When the snowball dance started, I made sure to go get a drink and use the bathroom, taking a considerable amount of time getting back. Using these methods, I made it through the dance without ever having to dance with anyone.

When I turned twelve, one of my first youth activities was a ward dance. Using my sneaky methods, I avoided dancing with a girl for a while—until Sister Johnson, one of the Young Women leaders, caught on to what I was doing. While strolling about in the middle of the dance floor, weaving in and out of dancing couples, I suddenly walked right into Sister Johnson (obviously she had stealthily aligned her position). With a big smile, she said, "Chas, have you danced with anyone yet?"

I knew I was doomed. My mind raced for a plan, but I knew it was too late. So after a few moments of hesitation, all I could say was, "Uh . . . no . . . not really."

Then she grabbed the first Laurel to walk by and said, "Shawna, would you like to dance with Chas?"

Being a mature sixteen-year-old, she took pity on this poor little deacon. "I'd love to!"

Feeling like a mouse caught in a trap, I stood there as she put her hands on my shoulders. I was shocked. What was I supposed to do now? I stood there stupidly.

"Put your hands on my waist," she instructed.

I couldn't believe this was happening. I was going to actually dance with this girl! I'd seen the other boys dancing, so I guess I knew I was supposed to put my hands on her waist, but I couldn't work up the courage to do it before the invitation came. I put my hands on her waist, and we rocked back and forth slightly, turning gradually in circles. The song was already half over by the time we'd started dancing, but that second half felt like the length of a whole album.

When the song finally ended, she thanked me for the dance, and I bolted. For the rest of the evening, I kept clear of that girl.

At home after the dance, Mom told me how Shawna had come up to her and Dad. "Your son is so cute! I had to tell him to put his hands on my hips!"

Turning purple at the thought that Mom and Dad knew that I had danced with a girl, I wormed off to my room.

What is it with adults? I thought. *Why do they feel it is their lot in life to get every deacon to fall in love at age twelve? I thought we couldn't even date till we were sixteen!* In my opinion, this commandment protected those poor pressured young people from having to scare themselves silly before their time.

It took me a while to understand what a crush was. All I knew was certain girls scared me, and I didn't know why. From that first dance on, I was deathly afraid of Shawna. She certainly wasn't my first crush, but she had been my first dance. For the next year or so,

I tried hard to avoid dances as much as possible, but it wasn't long before my stake had another youth dance.

I sharpened my skills for this dance and found ways to make it look from the sides of the dance floor like I was actually dancing with a girl. This worked for a while, until Sister Johnson found me again. Next thing I knew, I was dancing with another girl! Andrea was my age. In fact, she was in my Sunday school class. Gratefully, I wasn't nearly as afraid of her as I was Shawna, because I knew Andrea was also scared to death to dance. I'm not sure why knowing that helped, but it did.

It would be difficult to pinpoint when my attitude toward certain girls changed from avoidance at all cost to an interest in being near them. I suppose the fear never fully disappeared, since even when I was well into the dating stage of my life, I still freaked out to be anywhere in sight of a girl I was interested in. But there came a time when fear was overpowered by interest.

I think that kind of fear is normal for young teenagers. Their bodies and minds are going through changes that neither the teen nor their parents fully understand, and these changes lead to a powerful attraction to the opposite sex. For each person, this change will take on different forms.

Some young teenagers feel a desire to date by the time they are thirteen. Others don't have a desire until they are twenty. So why shouldn't we just start dating as soon as we feel the desire?

Avoid Pairing Off

The Lord is aware of our various levels of preparation, and He has instructed us to not even attempt the dating process before the age of sixteen. But what if we aren't "dating"? What if we're just holding hands and hanging out?

Ahem . . .

Well, see, that's dating. In fact, it's fairly serious dating, because not only are you spending time one-on-one, but it probably means you are being exclusive, which means you're not seeing other people.

The pamphlet *For the Strength of Youth* says simply, "Do not date until you are at least 16 years old."[1] President Spencer W. Kimball was even more specific in this counsel:

> You will do well to grow up as children, associating with both girls and boys for those first years. When you get in the teenage years, your social associations should still be general acquaintance with both boys and girls. Any dating or pairing off in social contacts should be postponed until at least the age of 16 or older, and even then there should be much judgment used in selections and in the seriousness.
>
> Young people should still limit the close contacts for several years, since the boy will be going on his mission when he is 19 years old. There should be limited contacts and certainly no approach to the intimate relationships involving sex. There must never be any sex of any kind prior to marriage.[2]

Any dating *or* pairing off should wait. Before you are of dateable age, you shouldn't be spending a lot of time one-on-one with someone of the opposite sex. You especially don't need to be physical (hand-holding, hugging, kissing, and so on) with anyone.

But even after you turn sixteen, you will need to "limit close contacts." I understand that to mean you shouldn't go steady at sixteen. Until you are old enough and mature enough to get married, your dating should be casual, fun, and *commitment-free*. That should help the guys relax.

It also means that physical contact should be *severely* limited. That should help the girls relax.

Actually, those things should help both girls *and* guys relax. Especially if you are under sixteen. You don't have to stress about that magical time when you are suddenly dateable. Really, turning sixteen just means that you can do group dates and school dances. Having a boyfriend or girlfriend should be reserved for the marriageable years, and you shouldn't have to stress about it in your mid-teens.

JUST SAY NO TO NC²

Have you ever heard of NC²? That was a term used in my generation, though there's probably some other term for it now. It stood for

Non-Committal-Cuddling. The idea was to be able to *act* like boy-friend and girlfriend without any commitment or date. An example might be snuggling or kissing someone during a big group movie night at someone's house—just for fun. Some feel that this is accept-able behavior as long as the two agree to it. All I have to say about that is . . . *wrongo, bongo!*

Talk about hypocritical! Words mean nothing when actions don't agree.

This is especially dangerous in the early teenage years, because you may not officially be "dating" this person. But if you have paired off somehow—"seeing each other" or "going together" or whatever bogus term your junior high uses—it is still dating, even if the word *date* is never used. In fact, you are more than dating; you are going steady, which is another word for courting. The only moral next step in the relationship is engagement, and early teenage years don't need that. Just remember behaviors that imply "she's mine" and "I'm hers" are intended for marriageable years, which means at *least* after high school. Just don't go there.

It helps to keep that information in mind before you turn six-teen, so when you do, you won't suddenly feel like you should have a boyfriend or girlfriend. You're not going from ineligible to mar-riageable.

WHAT YOU *CAN* DO NOW

So as a pre-sixteen, what do you do while waiting for those dateable years? Well, for one, you can work on becoming a better friend. The most basic element of marriage is friendship. In fact, friendship is more powerful and more important in a relationship than romance. During these early years, you shouldn't be practicing your romance skills anyway, so why not work on your friendship skills? And don't limit this to members of the opposite sex. If you don't work hard to develop your ability to become a good friend, no one will want to date you when you are old enough. But we'll talk more about friend-ship in the next chapter.

These years are also a great time to develop and strengthen your testimony. Your mind is in the process of growing and expanding at a rate that will never be matched for the rest of your life. The course you set now will set the direction and momentum of everything else you do—through time and eternity. If the idea of working on your testimony sounds boring to you, then you haven't been taking the right approach. If you think sitting in Sunday School is as interesting as the gospel gets, then I'm afraid you have been missing out!

Take seminary classes, go to firesides, get on the Internet, or go to your library to find youth talks by inspiring LDS speakers. But most of all, delve deep into the scriptures and pray diligently and sincerely to your Father in Heaven. If you think that process is boring, then you haven't tried it with real intent, and there's no better time to start than now. As you pray sincerely, study the scriptures diligently, and keep attending your Church meetings, you'll even notice that Sunday School is suddenly interesting. When that happens, life is so AWESOME! You'll even surprise yourself.

DEVELOP YOUR TALENTS

This is also a great time to work on developing your talents. As a young teenager, your body has just barely reached an amazing breakthrough in motor skills, muscle growth, and eye-hand coordination that makes it easy to learn skills and become really good at whatever you choose to do. You may find that suddenly you are much better at all kinds of sports. Develop those skills. Strengthen and refine them, if athletics is one of your interests.

Also, your mind has begun an expansion process that puts you in an ideal situation to develop your skills in art, music, computers, writing, building, and studying. It now only takes a little time for you to master a skill or become proficient in the knowledge of a favorite subject. Try out something you've always wanted to do. You'll learn fast. If you don't know what you want to do, try a couple things to see if you like them. You'll pick them up fast enough to keep from getting bored, and if you stick to it, you'll become really good.

Learn Self-Discipline Now

As part of this body and mind expansion, you are also developing a curious and powerful draw toward those members of the opposite sex. This is both normal and good—though sometimes frightening or overwhelming. You will experience temptation in ways that you couldn't have imagined five years ago. Because of this, you must be extremely careful what you do about your new feelings toward those around you. In fact, the best thing you can do is learn *now* how to control your reactions to your feelings.

Getting involved too early in the dating game (whether officially or unofficially) can interrupt the normal, proper development of social skills, emotional maturity, and personal character. This is the best time of life to learn and build your social and emotional discipline. Getting involved with someone in the early teenage years can create tendencies and habits that will be hard to break later.

Let's look at it from another angle—only in the past few years have you developed a powerful natural interest in the opposite sex. Those feelings and inclinations will increase for the next few years, and then they will stay for the rest of your life. After you are married, you will only have one person with whom you can righteously fulfill those attractions. There will be countless other people throughout your life who you will find physically attractive, but you can only follow through with those feelings with your spouse. You will spend most of your life suppressing and ignoring your attraction to other people. That is an absolutely invaluable ability and a challenging discipline that you must exercise if you want to have a chance of a happy family life. Right now, while those feelings are growing and developing, is the best time to learn discipline. If you're exercising strict discipline during these first seven or eight years of having those powerful feelings, you will develop the strength you need to withstand a lifetime of temptation.

If, however, you decide as soon as those feelings start coming, to act on them, then how strong will your discipline be after you are married?

Ah, you may think, *but I will have my spouse! I will have the girl of my dreams!* That's true, but your spouse isn't going to be with you everywhere you go. You will still see people at school and work. Besides, those twitterpated feelings that first got you together fade with time. This is not because your attraction to the opposite sex fades but because of time, familiarity, and aging with your spouse. Gratefully, those twitterpated feelings for your spouse are replaced with a more meaningful, committed, trusting love that surpasses the "crush" that got the two of you together. But if you have not developed the discipline to be faithful in action and thought or learned how to ignore your physical attraction to others, your marriage won't survive.

So develop that discipline early. Work on it now, while you are too young to date anyway. You will have many years to search for the perfect companion after high school, and for guys, after your mission.

NOTES

1. *For the Strength of Youth: Fulfilling Our Duty to God* (Salt Lake City: Intellectual Reserve, 2001), 24.
2. Spencer W. Kimball, "Marriage—The Proper Way," *New Era*, Feb. 1976, 5.

two

Get Some BFFs

Whether you recognize it or not, your friends have a tremendous impact on you.

Gordon B. Hinckley was talking directly to the youth of the church when he said:

> Choose your friends carefully. It is they who will lead you in one direction or the other. Everybody wants friends. Everybody needs friends. No one wishes to be without them. But never lose sight of the fact that it is your friends who will lead you along the paths that you will follow.
>
> While you should be friendly with all people, select with great care those whom you wish to have close to you. They will be your safeguards in situations where you may vacillate between choices, and you in turn may save them.[1]

You've probably heard a lot about peer pressure and how dangerous it can be. But it can actually be a very positive and good thing, if the pressure is to do what's right. Those kinds of friends are true friends. They want to see you succeed in life.

THE TRUE FRIEND

Often, when someone applies pressure to give in to temptation, it is simply their way of trying to feel better about their own sins. If everyone's doing it, they think they are justified. Some friend, eh? Do they really even care what happens to you? Sounds pretty selfish to me.

But when someone applies pressure that encourages you to do what's right, it is a clear indication that they care about you and want to see you happy.

Robert D. Hales of the Quorum of the Twelve taught this principle beautifully when he said:

> Do you know how to recognize a true friend? A real friend loves us and protects us.
>
> In recognizing a true friend we must look for two important elements in that friendship:
>
> A true friend makes it easier for us to live the gospel by being around him.
>
> Similarly, a true friend does not make us choose between his way and the Lord's way. A true friend will help us return with honor.
>
> By applying these two fundamental principles to our selection of friends, we can determine what kind of friends we will have and what kind of friend we will be.[2]

What a great test of friendship! Does this person make it easier to live the gospel? If so, they're a keeper! Someone who wants you to succeed and become better will rejoice when you do, and your friendship will become stronger every time you make a righteous choice.

Besides, like we talked about before, friendship is the basis of a good marriage. Two people, no matter how in love they are, would never be good marriage partners without becoming best friends first. And while you should not seek a potential dating partner yet, you can and should be learning to be a good friend. That skill will serve you throughout your life, especially when it's time to look for someone to marry.

Practice making friends with those who have high standards, who make it easier to live the gospel of Jesus Christ. Then when you're of dating age, you'll have already learned the most important social skills that are necessary for dating—kindness, trustworthiness, loyalty, worthiness, honesty, and integrity. Without those skills, you'll never be a good dating partner.

POPULARITY IS AN ILLUSION

There's a common misconception in the teenage years that friendship means popularity. Don't shoot for popularity. For most people, it's an illusion—kind of like a rainbow. The closer you get to it, the more it seems to disappear. But I can promise you—*promise you*—your lack of popularity in junior high and high school will have very little, if anything, to do with your future dating success. Popularity ends when high school is over. And according to the prophets, serious dating shouldn't start until after high school anyway.

Some teenagers are afraid that their opportunities for romantic love will be gone after high school because all the friends and prospects they have are *in* high school, and they know virtually no one out of high school. They fear that once they are out of high school, all those prospects will go their separate ways and most will be lost to them. It seems to them as if in high school they were in a wonderful (or horrid, depending on the individual) little aquarium with hundreds of potentials and that when they are dumped out to sea, the world will be too big to find anyone.

Actually, you'll just be dumped into a different aquarium with a whole new batch of potentials. Why? Because your workplace will have potentials, your college classes will have potentials, and your ward will have potentials (especially if you go to a young single adult ward).

It doesn't take long to get to know people from a new group, especially if you spent your pre-sixteen years practicing making new friends. However dorky you were in high school, starting in these new areas of work, college, institute, and so on are a great opportunity to start over. Besides, after high school, that compartmentalization (the nerds versus the popular, dorks versus athletes) almost completely goes away, believe it or not. And your new opportunities give you a chance to show who you really are outside of high school labels. It's just a matter of being involved and attending activities—but we'll get into that in a later chapter.

Hugh W. Pinnock of the Seventy, speaking about friendships, taught: "Choose your friends carefully. Associate with young men and young women who will assist you to be responsible. Help your friends decide to go on missions, to attend Church meetings, and to enjoy righteous activities. You who are sixteen and older and are dating, make sure the girls you date are just as good when you return them to their homes as when you picked them up."[3]

You could take that last statement and say it about friends. Make sure you are as good after hanging out with friends as you were before. Also, make sure your friends are just as good after they've hung out with you as they were before. In fact, why not help them be better by hanging out with you? According to Elder Hales, that's what a real friend is anyway.

NOTES

1. Gordon B. Hinckley, "A Prophet's Counsel and Prayer for Youth," *New Era*, Jan. 2001, 4.
2. Robert D. Hales, "The Aaronic Priesthood: Return with Honor," *Ensign*, May 1990, 39.
3. Hugh W. Pinnock, "Your Personal Checklist for a Successful Eternal Flight," *Ensign*, Nov. 1993, 40.

three

While You're Waiting . . .

If you are the kind of person who has no desire to date before the age of sixteen, you are fortunate indeed. You have probably already figured out that there is more to life than the opposite sex. But if you are one who is waiting anxiously for that golden year of opportunity, here are some ideas for things to do in the meantime.

It helps to recognize that before you can date, you must become a good, dateable person. Likewise, before you marry someday, you have to become the type of person someone will want to marry—and not just *any* someone but the *best* someone possible. Your teenage years are the ideal time to develop the traits and attributes that a good spouse will want. In the priesthood session of general conference, President Gordon B. Hinckley addressed the young men and said,

> The girl you marry will take a terrible chance on you. She will give her all to the young man she marries. He will largely determine the remainder of her life. She will even surrender her name to his name. . . .
>
> You have a tremendous obligation toward the girl you marry. Perhaps you are not thinking much of that now. But the time isn't far away when you will think of it, and now is the time to prepare for that most important day of your lives when you take unto yourself a wife and companion equal with you before the Lord.
>
> That obligation begins with absolute loyalty. As the old Church

of England ceremony says, you will marry her "for richer or for poorer, in sickness and in health, for better or for worse." She will be yours and yours alone, regardless of the circumstances of your lives. You will be hers and hers alone. There can be eyes for none other. There must be absolute loyalty, undeviating loyalty one to another. Hopefully you will marry her forever, in the house of the Lord, under the authority of the everlasting priesthood. Through all the days of your lives, you must be as true one to another as the polar star.

The girl you marry can expect you to come to the marriage altar absolutely clean. She can expect you to be a young man of virtue in thought and word and deed.

I plead with you boys tonight to keep yourselves free from the stains of the world.[1]

Have you ever thought of your dating preparation in terms of what your future spouse would want? What kind of person are you becoming for the person you will someday marry? The biggest key is to keep yourself 100 percent clean. *One hundred percent.* No exceptions. Don't play around with pornography or inappropriate video games or movies. Why? Because not only do they damage the spirit within you, but you are at a terribly impressionable stage of life. Whether you believe it or not, the things you do now will set a pattern for the rest of your life. If you pick up swearing now, it will be very hard to stop later. If you begin drinking, doing drugs, or developing a bad temper now, you are setting yourself up to a life of slavery and suffering. Do you really want to risk losing your chance for a wonderful spouse by getting involved in these things now? Or worse, do you want to risk hurting a future spouse by letting these things take over your life?

No matter what happens, *keep yourself clean!* It is *so* worth it, I promise you. Take President Hinckley's counsel seriously:

> And so, my dear young men, you may not think seriously about it now. But the time will come when you will fall in love. It will occupy all of your thoughts and be the stuff of which your dreams are made. Make yourself worthy of the loveliest girl in all the world. Keep yourself worthy through all the days of your life. Be good and true and kind one to another. There is so much of bitterness in the world. There is so much of pain and sorrow that come of angry

words. There is so much of tears that follow disloyalty. But there can be so much of happiness if there is an effort to please and an overwhelming desire to make comfortable and happy one's companion.

When all is said and done, this is what the gospel is about. The family is a creation of God . . .

Young men, now is the time to prepare for the future. And in that future for most of you is a beautiful young woman whose greatest desire is to bond with you in a relationship that is eternal and everlasting.

You will know no greater happiness than that found in your home. You will have no more serious obligation than that which you face in your home. The truest mark of your success in life will be the quality of your marriage.[2]

In your efforts to avoid dating prematurely, make sure you don't confuse the letter of the law with the spirit of the law. Of course you should not date before your sixteen, but that doesn't mean it's okay to pair off with someone you like as long as it's in a public or non-dating situation. The spirit of the law is to avoid getting involved with any one person before the proper time, whether it's a date or not.

Brad Wilcox, a school teacher and a bishop, told this story:

"It's not like we were on a date, Bishop," said Paul. "We were just hanging out." Fifteen-year-old Paul was trying to explain why he was having moral problems with a young lady whom he had never "dated." When the bishop spoke with the young lady, she, like Paul, failed to grasp the seriousness of what they had done because, after all, they weren't "dating."

Immorality is immorality whenever it happens or wherever it happens. Despite what is shown in movies or sung in love songs, immorality always results in undesirable consequences. When it comes to staying clean, sometimes hanging out can be even more dangerous than dating because young people don't have their guards up. They are vulnerable to temptation and experimentation because they feel more comfortable, relaxed, and safe than they do in formal situations.[3]

Have you ever thought about what you will someday say when your fourteen-year-old child comes to you and asks you why she can't date before she's sixteen? What will you say when she asks, "But didn't you date before you were sixteen?" Wouldn't it be so much simpler to be able to say, "No, I didn't, and I'm very grateful I didn't," than, "Yes, but I changed." Kids are smart. They will make your life miserable if you even attempt to prevent them from doing something you once did. They won't care that you changed. In their mind, they will probably change someday too. That's even more dangerous.

NOTES

1. Hinckley, "Living Worthy of the Girl You Will Someday Marry," 49.
2. Ibid.
3. Brad Wilcox, "Just Hanging Out," *New Era*, Aug. 2001, 8.

Old Enough to Date . . .
but not too seriously

Let no man despise thy youth; but be thou an
example of the believers, in word, in conversation,
in charity, in spirit, in faith, in purity.
—1 Timothy 4:12

four

Sweet Sixteen!

S weet sixteen and never been dated.

You did it! You made it to sixteen alive! Believe me, that's a major accomplishment, and if your parents are still surviving, then it's an even bigger accomplishment. Have you ever wondered why everyone says the teen years are so rough—both for you and your parents?

Your body is changing, your focus is changing, your opinions are changing, your interactions with your parents are changing, and the way you see the world is changing. It feels as though the entire world is changing—and it is. But most of the change is taking place in you, and it's important to recognize that. Did you know that the changes you are going through are part of the plan of salvation? Did you know that God intended for you to go through a great deal of change during your teenage years? Even your overwhelming need for independence is part of God's plan. These changes are part of your eternal progression.

With all these changes, there comes a strong sense of independence in which you want to make your own choices. That is important, and very good. Our Heavenly Father has clearly stated in the scriptures that agency is an essential part of His plan. You need to make your own choices. You cannot be saved if someone else has forced you to do what's right—not even your parents. While they may have strict rules and insist that you follow them, the choice is ultimately yours. You are a child of God, and as such, it is essential you make conscious choices for yourself.

That also means that no matter how good or bad your parents are—no matter how well they teach you or how badly they neglect you, ultimately your success, in life and in eternity, is up to you. Ultimately, you decide what kind of life you will have. And you must decide what kind of person you will be.

If you do not make conscious decisions for yourself, then someone else will make your decisions for you, and it won't be Heavenly Father. He has already promised not to force you to heaven. He has provided all the knowledge, tools, and resources necessary for you to return to Him safely. He loves you so much that He will let you be the one to decide whether or not to follow Him.

So who will try to make decisions for you? Let me give you a hint: he has already attempted to destroy your freedom to choose. He tried to destroy all your chances to become a free agent—and failed. He has intention to destroy your agency through slavery to emotions, appetites, passions, fears, pride, addiction, or whatever it takes. Know who I'm talking about? That's right, ol' scratch himself—satan. You may notice that we didn't capitalize the name: he doesn't deserve it; he's not a proper pronoun or anything else proper—he's just there, and he hates you. And he hates me too—he's out to get us all. Why? Well, he's evil, he's jealous, and he wants more than anything to spite God and make you miserable. All in all, he's got serious issues.

Even so, *do not underestimate* him. He has had thousands of years of practice making God's children miserable, and he knows what it takes to bring you down. While talking about a number of satan's tactics, Nephi said:

> And others will he pacify, and lull them away into carnal security, that they will say: All is well in Zion; yea, Zion prospereth, all is well—and thus the devil cheateth their souls, and leadeth them away carefully down to hell.
>
> And behold, others he flattereth away, and telleth them there is

no hell; and he saith unto them: I am no devil, for there is none—and thus he whispereth in their ears, until he grasps them with his awful chains, from whence there is no deliverance. (2 Nephi 28:21–22)

Here's what President James E. Faust said about him:

The First Presidency described Satan: "He is working under such perfect disguise that many do not recognize either him or his methods. There is no crime he would not commit, no debauchery he would not set up, no plague he would not send, no heart he would not break, no life he would not take, no soul he would not destroy. He comes as a thief in the night; he is a wolf in sheep's clothing." Satan is the world's master in the use of flattery, and he knows the great power of speech, a power his servants often employ. He has always been one of the great forces of the world. [1]

In fact, if he were given the opportunity to do everything he would normally have the power to do, he would make you a slave without you having any say in the matter. He is that evil. So why can't he do it? Very simply, because God has put up certain barriers that he cannot cross. God put up enough barriers to keep the choice in your hands. Satan can still influence you, whisper to you, lie to you, persuade and frighten you, but he cannot force you.

Paul said:

There hath no temptation taken you but such as is common to man: but God is faithful, who will not suffer you to be tempted above that ye are able; but will with the temptation also make a way to escape, that ye may be able to bear it. (1 Corinthians 10:13)

Oh, good, so God has provided a way to escape—He has created a barrier. It is a narrow escape, but He has provided a way. But what is that barrier? If you do not know it, you might not be using it—and to not use God's barrier is terribly dangerous. So what is it?

Alma said:

But that ye would humble yourselves before the Lord, and call on his holy name, and watch and pray continually, that ye may not be tempted above that which ye can bear, and thus be led by the Holy Spirit, becoming humble, meek, submissive, patient, full of love and all long-suffering. (Alma 13:28)

Humble yourself and PRAY! Without prayer, we would be unable to stop satan from taking control of our lives. Prayer is satan's biggest barrier and his biggest annoyance—which is why it is so good to pray when you experience temptation. Satan hates it, and usually leaves.

The Lord has said:

> Pray always, that you may come off conqueror; yea, that you may conquer Satan, and that you may escape the hands of the servants of Satan that do uphold his work. (D&C 10:5)

While prayer may be the greatest barrier, God has given you many things to protect you against the power of satan. He has provided church meetings, youth leaders, parents (yes, parents really are a *good* thing, and you know it!), the scriptures (read them, read them, read them!), and service opportunities. It's very difficult for satan to influence you when you are willingly using these tools. Not only do these things protect you, but they are also catalysts to your happiness, success, and fulfillment. They will promote strength, wisdom, courage, and self-esteem.

Don't forget—the choice is *yours*. God has insisted that it be so. And during your teenage years, your sense of choice and independence is increased in order to encourage you to make conscious right choices. Will you be tempted to make choices that lead to addiction? Of course. Remember, satan would love to destroy you here and now, and turn you into an addict and a slave. But God loves you enough to protect your agency and leave the choice in your hands.

There are few subjects with which satan has given more attention than the subject of marriage, family, and sexual relations. These are something of his specialty:

Bruce C. Hafen noted:

> It's now simply a fact that most of those who write and most of those who produce today's movies, TV programs, and popular music, as well as those who set the editorial policies of many magazines, believe that sex outside of marriage is really quite harmless. On this particular subject of sexual morality, I honestly believe our society is within the grip of the evil one.

Can you see why the Brethren tell us to stay away from X- and R-rated movies? Can you see why they plead with us to avoid drugs, alcohol, vulgar music, and the other products of the carnal environment that now surrounds us almost as water surrounds the fish of the sea? These aren't trivial things. If the H-bomb symbolizes our age, we are playing now not just with fire, but with nuclear power. The prince of darkness has dragged out the heavy artillery.[2]

You can choose to act contrary to the Lord's plan. The Lord has allowed you that right to choose, but you should know that if you choose to turn away from God's plan, you are choosing to hand your agency over to satan. Once you take down God's protective barriers, satan will take control of your life. He will do all he can to convince you that it is you who is in control—all the while working you into addictions and habits that will destroy your life and all your chances for happiness. Never underestimate satan, and never fall into his traps.

NOTES

1. James E. Faust, "The Forces That Will Save Us," *Ensign*, Jan. 2007, 2–7.
2. Bruce C. Hafen, "The Gospel and Romantic Love," *New Era*, Feb. 2002, 10.

five

Seriously?

We often subconsciously think of standards as a thing for youth, but clearly the commandments of God do not change with age. The only thing that changes as we mature is our preparedness to make the transition from one phase of life into another, such as going from not dating (pre-sixteen) to casual dating (sixteen to eighteen), and then from casual dating to serious dating. During your high school years, you don't need to pair off. Not only are you unprepared for the commitments of a steady relationship, but by keeping your dating casual and light, you avoid a great deal of moral temptation. By saving serious dating until you are mature enough to marry, you save yourself from heartbreak of many kinds.

Boyd K. Packer spoke out very directly about this:

> When you are old enough, you ought to start dating. It is good for young men and young women to learn to know and to appreciate one another. It is good for you to go to games and dances and picnics, to do all of the young things. We encourage our young people to date. We encourage you to set high standards of dating.
>
> When are you old enough? Maturity may vary from individual to individual, but we are convinced that dating should not even begin until you are 16. And then, ideal dating is on a group basis.

Stay in group activities; don't pair off. Avoid steady dating. Steady dating is courtship, and surely the beginning of courtship ought to be delayed until you have emerged from your teens.[1]

The time from sixteen until you are of a marriageable age is remarkably short, no matter how long it feels to you now. And you have a lot to learn in those dateable but not marriageable years. It would be better not to date at all than to get yourself into trouble. This is a learning period. If you spoil it with sin, you may prevent the opportunities to date those with high standards when you are of marriageable age. Making a wrong choice now may prevent you from being able to make the right choice later.

Robert D. Hales said: "Avoid having a relationship where there is talk or behavior that is sexually oriented. Avoid being alone with your date or staying out too late. You are both responsible to help each other maintain the sanctity of the priesthood and womanhood and to protect each other's honor and virtue."[2]

This is a great time to sample the dating game. I say sample because you really aren't fully playing the game until you are marriageable. Marriageable means you are in a position in life where you could rightfully marry if you found the right person. So use this little bit of time to learn the social skills that you will need to play the real game later.

Spencer W. Kimball emphasized the importance of this when he counseled:

> Every boy should have been saving money for his mission and be free from any and all entanglements so he will be worthy. When he is returned from his mission . . . , he should feel free to begin to get acquainted and to date. When he has found the right young woman, there should be a proper temple marriage. One can have all the blessings if he is in control and takes the experiences in proper turn: first some limited, social, get-acquainted contacts, then his mission, then his courting, then his temple marriage and his schooling and his family, then his life's work. In any other sequence he could run into difficulty.[3]

One of the ways you can establish a tradition of good family life is to keep your focus on the stage of life you are in now. All of your natural inclinations will have an opportunity to be satisfied in time. Patience will do a lot to prepare you for marriage. Exercise strong self-discipline and keep your focus on being the best you can at your present state of life. Work hard in school, and develop your body, mind, and spirit. Take the opportunity to participate in positive, appropriate social activities so you can practice interacting with the opposite sex in a spiritually-safe environment. You are not trying to find an eternal companion yet, but you're learning needed skills to use for that search.

Robert D. Hales said:

> Your teenage years are not the time to make that decision [of who to marry], but proper dating will help you prepare to make that decision when it is appropriate. Dating will give you opportunities to develop social skills that will help you become confident and attractive to the young women you date. You'll come to understand and be attracted to those with the qualities and characteristics that will be important to you in an eternal companion. Proper dating will also help you be worthy and prepared to marry in the temple for time and all eternity the right person at the right time.[4]

Have you ever thought about the fact that what you do with your life now—your goals for a future family, your general approach to life—may affect the trends of society in the next generation? You are literally shaping the future. If you encourage the trends toward early dating, your children will grow up in the society that has adopted that practice as a norm. And they may want to date even earlier than you did. If you push the trends toward discipline, righteousness, honesty, and patience, your children will someday grow up in the society that has learned to live by those trends. Which would you rather your children experience?

Brent A. Barlow, who was a professor of marriage, family, and human development at BYU, explained:

> There is nationwide concern about the next generation regarding marriage. I identify particularly the people from the ages 16 to 26 because some of the best thinkers in this nation have said, "As

goes the next generation, so goes the nation." What you do regarding marriage and family will determine a lot about the future of this country. We are at a crossroad in the United States. The trends that have been established during the last four decades regarding marriage and family have contributed to the demise of marriage and family, but there are some indications that, nationwide, your generation is changing and is putting marriage and family as a top priority. So we are very interested to see which way you are going to go.[5]

NOTES

1. Boyd K. Packer, "You're in the Driver's Seat," *New Era*, Jun. 2004, 8.
2. Young Men General Presidency, "To the Young Men on Dating," *New Era*, Apr. 2010, 6–7.
3. Kimball, "Marriage—The Proper Way," 5.
4. Young Men General Presidency, "To the Young Men on Dating," 6–7.
5. Brent A. Barlow, "Marriage is Ordained of God (D&C 49:15)," in *Brigham Young University 1999–2000 Speeches*, 12 Oct. 1999.

Marriageable Age

Who can find a virtuous woman?
For her price is far above rubies.
—Proverbs 31:10

six

~

Live It Up

When, really, can you call yourself totally marriageable? One way to know is to ask yourself, "If I were to meet the right person, and we fell in love this month, would now be a good stage of life for me to get married?" If you can answer yes, then you are probably of marriageable age. Either way, if you are a girl out of high school or a boy back from his mission, then most likely, you are of marriageable age. Beyond that, it depends on your own maturity—which grows as you dive fully into life.

So what do you do now? You spent sixteen years being told, "NO!" and a few more years with, "Not too seriously." Now you are being told, "Get married!" It's that "stages of life" thing we talked about earlier. You've now entered a new one, and there are many things to consider. No pressure, but remember how the "most important decision" is who you will marry? Yeah, well, it's time to work on discovering the answer to that question. Pray hard, because here you go!

ENJOY THE JOURNEY

Before diving too deep into the meat of marriageable age dating, here are some words of comfort from Pat and Jeffrey R. Holland:

Jeff: Quite apart from the matter of school or missions or marriage or whatever, life ought to be enjoyed at every stage of our experience and should not be hurried and wrenched and truncated and torn to fit an unnatural schedule which you have predetermined but which may not be the Lord's personal plan for you at all. As we look back with you today, we realize we have probably rushed too many things and been too anxious and too urgent for too much of our life, and perhaps you are already guilty of the same thing. We probably all get caught thinking real life is still ahead of us, still a little farther down the road.

Pat: Don't wait to live. Obviously, life for all of us began a long time ago—twenty-two years longer for us than for you—and the sand is falling through that hourglass as steadily as the sun rises and rivers run to the sea. Don't wait for life to gallop in and sweep you off your feet. It is a quieter, more pedestrian visitor than that. In a church which understands more about time and its relationship to eternity than any other, we of all people ought to savor every moment, ought to enjoy the time of preparation before marriage, filling it full of all the truly good things of life—one of the most valuable of which is a university education."[1]

So enjoy this new stage of life. It will be a grand adventure. Don't dwell too much on the past or wallow in the pity of what you don't yet have. Enjoy your life every day. If you don't find yourself generally happy, then you are doing something wrong. If it's unworthiness, fix it. If it's not, evaluate what it is that is making your life unhappy, and determine to get a new perspective: a spiritual, optimistic perspective that focuses on where you are, and what you're doing. Make the most out of every moment, occasionally asking yourself, "What is the best thing I can be doing right now?" and then have the courage to do it.

Happy Singles Make Happy Marrieds

Though it may annoy you to hear it, you will likely hear some married couples say, "Oh, just be glad you're still single, because when you get married and the kids come along, things gets rough." When they say that, just smile and say, "Don't worry, I love life."

What those people forget is that happy singles make happy marrieds, and happy marrieds make happy parents. If you had asked those people what they thought about singlehood while they had it, they'd probably say they hated it. So the key is to love life where you are, including the search for an eternal companion. It can be rough, but love it! Don't get so attached to it that you're not ready to move on when the time comes, but love every stage of life, always preparing for the next. Focus on living in the present.

NOTE

1. Jeffrey R. and Patricia T. Holland, "Some Things We Have Learned—Together," in *Brigham Young University 1984–85 Speeches*, 15 Jan. 1985.

~

seven

Alma's Dating Advice

One morning I got to school early in the morning before classes started. I had been home from my mission for a while, and I wanted to get on with my life. I wanted to get married and have a family. I had prayed and fasted for help in seeking out a companion.

None of my dating experiences so far had worked out (and there hadn't been many), and I didn't have my eye on anyone as a dating prospect at the moment.

Single adult life can be tough. Especially when you decide it's time to seek out a partner. I was both eager and apprehensive about diving headlong into the dating game. I had heard so many horror stories and had experienced enough of backfired crushes to know that it's a rocky road.

But I think what frightened me the most was that I felt like I knew virtually nothing about developing a relationship with a girl. I felt clumsy and ugly. I felt like a born loner when it came to girls. I could usually talk to them okay, but somehow I seemed to radiate an aura of "just friends." Those who I could talk to easily never seemed to even consider the idea that I might want to ask them out. I felt like the quintessential acquaintance—someone you know, perhaps talk to occasionally, but never consider a potential partner. It seemed to me that getting past that casualness would be like trying to penetrate the sound barrier—I would most likely crash and burn in the attempt.

Walking through the empty halls of the school, I decided to get out my Book of Mormon and read, hoping that by feeling the Spirit I would feel better about myself. Not wanting to become a spectacle if other students walked by, I found an empty classroom and sat down at a desk.

I opened to Alma 32. That had always been one of my favorite chapters, and my severe lack of dating success was compelling me to be humble. Maybe it could offer some help. I prayed for guidance and began to read.

I will say up front that even though the things I felt and learned inspired me, they cannot, and should not, be considered an interpretation of the verses—I didn't feel that they were then, and I don't feel so now. I don't think that was the intent of the experience, but I will share what I felt at that time, as it profoundly affected my attitude and approach to dating.

As I read Alma 32:26–43, something changed. The change was primarily in my mind, I know, but it was as though a transfer of learning was happening as I read, and I felt that the Lord was giving me a new perspective on my situation and on dating in general.

First I read the verses as they stand:

26 Now, as I said concerning faith—that it was not a perfect knowledge—even so it is with my words. Ye cannot know of their surety at first, unto perfection, any more than faith is a perfect knowledge.

27 But behold, if ye will awake and arouse your faculties, even to an experiment upon my words, and exercise a particle of faith, yea, even if ye can no more than desire to believe, let this desire work in you, even until ye believe in a manner that ye can give place for a portion of my words.

28 Now, we will compare the word unto a seed. Now, if ye give place, that a seed may be planted in your heart, behold, if it be a true seed, or a good seed, if ye do not cast it out by your unbelief, that ye will resist the Spirit of the Lord, behold, it will begin to swell within your breasts; and when you feel these swelling motions, ye will begin to say within yourselves—It must needs be that this is a good seed, or that the word is good, for it beginneth to enlarge my soul; yea, it

beginneth to enlighten my understanding, yea, it beginneth to be delicious to me.

29 Now behold, would not this increase your faith? I say unto you, Yea; nevertheless it hath not grown up to a perfect knowledge.

30 But behold, as the seed swelleth, and sprouteth, and beginneth to grow, then you must needs say that the seed is good; for behold it swelleth, and sprouteth, and beginneth to grow. And now, behold, will not this strengthen your faith? Yea, it will strengthen your faith: for ye will say I know that this is a good seed; for behold it sprouteth and beginneth to grow.

31 And now, behold, are ye sure that this is a good seed? I say unto you, Yea; for every seed bringeth forth unto its own likeness.

32 Therefore, if a seed groweth it is good, but if it groweth not, behold it is not good, therefore it is cast away.

33 And now, behold, because ye have tried the experiment, and planted the seed, and it swelleth and sprouteth, and beginneth to grow, ye must needs know that the seed is good.

34 And now, behold, is your knowledge perfect? Yea, your knowledge is perfect in that thing, and your faith is dormant; and this because you know, for ye know that the word hath swelled your souls, and ye also know that it hath sprouted up, that your understanding doth begin to be enlightened, and your mind doth begin to expand.

35 O then, is not this real? I say unto you, Yea, because it is light; and whatsoever is light, is good, because it is discernible, therefore ye must know that it is good; and now behold, after ye have tasted this light is your knowledge perfect?

36 Behold I say unto you, Nay; neither must ye lay aside your faith, for ye have only exercised your faith to plant the seed that ye might try the experiment to know if the seed was good.

37 And behold, as the tree beginneth to grow, ye will say: Let us nourish it with great care, that it may get root, that it may grow up, and bring forth fruit unto us. And now behold, if ye nourish it with much care it will get root, and grow up, and bring forth fruit.

38 But if ye neglect the tree, and take no thought for its nourishment, behold it will not get any root; and when the heat of the sun cometh and scorcheth it, because it hath no root it withers away, and ye pluck it up and cast it out.

39 Now, this is not because the seed was not good, neither is it because the fruit thereof would not be desirable; but it is because

your ground is barren, and ye will not nourish the tree, therefore ye cannot have the fruit thereof.

40 And thus, if ye will not nourish the word, looking forward with an eye of faith to the fruit thereof, ye can never pluck of the fruit of the tree of life.

41 But if ye will nourish the word, yea, nourish the tree as it beginneth to grow, by your faith with great diligence, and with patience, looking forward to the fruit thereof, it shall take root; and behold it shall be a tree springing up unto everlasting life.

42 And because of your diligence and your faith and your patience with the word in nourishing it, that it may take root in you, behold, by and by ye shall pluck the fruit thereof, which is most precious, which is sweet above all that is sweet, and which is white above all that is white, yea, and pure above all that is pure; and ye shall feast upon this fruit even until ye are filled, that ye hunger not, neither shall ye thirst.

43 Then, my brethren, ye shall reap the rewards of your faith, and your diligence, and patience, and long-suffering, waiting for the tree to bring forth fruit unto you.

It occurred to me that while this chapter was intended as a lecture on faith and obtaining a testimony of Christ, the same development may apply to other areas of truth. In my case, I was seeking love—true love—and eventually marriage. I wanted to learn how to start and build a relationship with a girl. So as an experiment, I changed the wording:

26 Now, as I said concerning love—that it was not a perfect knowledge of whom you should marry—even so it is with dating. Ye cannot know of a surety at first, unto perfection, who to marry, any more than love is a perfect knowledge of whom you should marry.

I couldn't simply be *told* who to date and marry without doing *my part*. I had to actively and prayerfully search.

27 But behold, if ye will awake and arouse your faculties, even to an experiment of dating someone, and exercise a particle of love, yea, even if ye can no more than desire to love, let this desire work in you, even until ye are sufficiently interested that ye can give place for the possibility of dating this person.

Hmm . . . this sounded familiar. I certainly wanted to begin dating, and I didn't know who to ask out. Maybe I should simply look for someone who meets the very basic criteria necessary (she's a member of the Church and temple worthy) and then exercise just enough interest in her to consider the possibility of dating her. I decided I could handle that.

> 28 Now, we will compare love unto a seed. Now, if ye give place, that the seed of love may be planted in your heart, behold, if it be a true seed of love, if ye do not cast it out by your distrust or irresponsibility, that ye will resist the spirit of love, behold, it will begin to swell within your breasts; and when you feel these swelling motions, ye will begin to say within yourself—It must needs be that this is a good seed, or that the relationship is good, for it beginneth to enlarge my soul; yea, it beginneth to enlighten my understanding, yea, it beginneth to be delicious to me.

Love is like a seed. If I begin dating a girl that I might be able to develop interest in, give place in my heart for love to grow, and treat her right, and if she does the same—if she considers that this relationship might work—then feelings of interest will grow inside me and develop into something deeper. Those feelings will lead me to want to be better and help me to understand and confide in her, and I will enjoy the feeling of being with her. That "deliciousness" might be called infatuation.

> 29 Now behold, would not this increase your feelings of love? I say unto you, Yea; nevertheless it hath not grown up to a perfect eternal love.
> 30 But behold, as your feelings swell, and sprout, and begin to grow, then you must needs say that the relationship is working; for behold it swelleth, and sprouteth, and beginneth to grow. And now, behold, will not this strengthen your love? Yea, it will strengthen your love: for ye will say I know that this is a good relationship; for behold it sprouteth and beginneth to grow.

Infatuation can certainly grow into love. It takes time, effort, and persistence, but it can grow into love. It was important for me to remember that this same process must be happening for the girl too, if it is to develop into true love. Most people understand these basic principles and will be willing to at least try one date's worth of the experiment.

31 And now, behold, are ye sure that this is a good relationship? I say unto you, Yea; for every seed bringeth forth unto its own likeness.

32 Therefore, if a relationship groweth it is good, but if it groweth not, behold it is not good, therefore it is cast away.

33 And now, behold, because ye have tried the experiment, and planted the seed, and it swelleth and sprouteth, and beginneth to grow, ye must needs know that the relationship is good.

34 And now, behold, is your knowledge of whether or not you could have a lasting relationship with this person perfect? Yea, your knowledge is perfect in that thing, and your infatuation is dormant; and this because you know, for ye know that the relationship hath swelled your souls, and ye also know that it hath sprouted up, that your understanding doth begin to be enlightened, and your mind doth begin to expand.

35 O then, is not this real? I say unto you, Yea, because it is light; and whatsoever is light, is good, because it is discernible, therefore ye must know that it is good; and now behold, after ye have tasted this light is your knowledge perfect that this is the person you *should* marry?

36 Behold I say unto you, Nay; neither must ye lay aside your love, for ye have only exercised your love to plant the seed that ye might try the experiment to know if the relationship could be good—if it has potential.

37 And behold, as your love begins to grow, ye will say: Let us nourish it with great care, that it may get root, that it may grow up, and bring forth fruit unto us. And now behold, if ye nourish it with much care it will get root, and grow up, and bring forth fruit.

38 But if ye neglect the relationship, and take no thought for its nourishment, behold it will not get any root; and when the heat of the sun cometh and scorcheth it, because it hath no root it withers away, and ye pluck it up and cast it out.

39 Now, this is not because the relationship's potential was not good, neither is it because marriage to this person would not be desirable; but it is because your ground is barren, and ye will not nourish the relationship, therefore ye cannot marry this person.

Clearly if I begin dating a girl and we don't communicate well, or she shows no interest in me, then things aren't going to work out. Or perhaps we communicate well, and we treat each other well, but physical and emotional interest is lacking. Perhaps it is also not the kind of relationship that can grow into true romantic love.

Perhaps the relationship has great potential, has all the important elements—including that spark of infatuation—and there is no reason things shouldn't work. Yet if I stop trying, if I get lazy about building and strengthening the relationship, it can't grow. Feeding a loving relationship takes a lifetime, perhaps eternal life, in order to survive. So if I can't learn to continue feeding the relationship, it can't last.

But let's say things *are* going well, and both parties are eager to see the success of the relationship. How do we now turn infatuation and hope into love?

> 40 And thus, if ye will not nourish the relationship, looking forward with an eye of faith to the possibility of marriage, ye can never pluck of the fruit of eternal marriage.
>
> 41 But if ye will nourish the love, yea, nourish the relationship as it beginneth to grow, by your faith with great diligence, and with patience, looking forward to the possibility of marriage, it shall take root; and behold it shall become a marriage springing up unto everlasting life.
>
> 42 And because of your diligence and your love and your faith and your patience with the relationship in nourishing it, that it may take root in you, behold, by and by ye shall fall in love, and get married in the temple, and the blessings thereof are most precious, and sweet above all that is sweet, and white above all that is white, yea, and pure above all that is pure; and ye shall feast upon these blessings even until ye are filled, that ye hunger not, neither shall ye thirst.
>
> 43 Then, my brethren, ye shall reap the rewards of your faith, and your love, and your diligence, and patience, and long-suffering, waiting for the relationship to bring forth true love unto you.

Now I have no doubt that if you were to follow the same substitutive pattern, you could find greater insight than I did, but to me, this experiment was a great lesson in love. Love is not something that you simply decide to do and then do it. When you are looking for an eternal marriage partner, you cannot just be pointed to the right girl and told to go propose. Love is an attribute. Even romantic love must be developed like every other attribute. And how do I develop it? By placing faith in the possibilities, exercising *acts* of love, and persisting in patience. It is not an equation, but a process, just like the growth of a seed is a process.

Was I ready for such a move? No. Is anyone ready? I don't think so. That's why we need the Savior. He knows us perfectly, and he knows our potential perfectly. He will help us learn how to date, how to love, how to build an eternal relationship. He's the perfect dating advisor and the perfect healer of heartbreaks. Stay close to Him. Stay *very* close to Him!

Jeffrey R. Holland counseled:

> Of course such Christlike staying power in romance and marriage requires more than any of us really have. It requires something more, an endowment from heaven. Remember Mormon's promise: that such love—the love we each yearn for and cling to—is "bestowed" upon "true followers of Christ." You want capability, safety, and security in dating and romance, in married life and eternity? Be a true disciple of Jesus. Be a genuine, committed, word-and-deed Latter-day Saint. Believe that your faith has everything to do with your romance, because it does. You separate dating from discipleship at your peril. Or, to phrase that more positively, Jesus Christ, the Light of the World, is the only lamp by which you can successfully see the path of love and happiness for you and for your sweetheart.[1]

The unique thing about romantic love is it cannot be fully developed without the reciprocation of the partner. I can think of no other attribute that requires two people in order to be genuine and complete (aside from you and the Lord). Romantic love can only reach its fullest state if he loves her completely and she loves him completely. Anything less is insufficient for marriage.

You may notice also that this experiment does not mention anything about what *type* of person to look for or even whether this person is worthy of your love. This lesson is teaching the basic concept of how to fall in love. It's possible to fall in love with someone you shouldn't marry, but that is another discussion. The point here is that anyone willing to exercise a particle of love, even if he can do no more than desire to love, let that *desire* work in him to a point that he is willing to actually *do* something about it.

As this understanding came to me, I realized from my standpoint that I simply needed to act on my desire. I needed to take the next step. Perhaps I needed to go to more activities and socials. Perhaps I needed to find a decent girl and ask her out. Hoping and praying for it would not be enough. I had to exercise enough interest in a girl to talk to her, to get to know her, and to ask her out. That would be how I plant the seed. How could I even hope to know the condition of my ground without planting a seed in it? It was time to turn my hopes into action.

NOTE

1. Jeffrey R. Holland, "How Do I Love Thee?," *Speeches*, 15 Feb. 2000.

eight

A Date with Tiffany

Though my intent was to start dating right away, it took me some time to decide who to ask out. Being deathly afraid to ask anyone on a date, I waited awhile.

I had been working at Deseret Book for a number of months and gradually started taking notice of one of my coworkers. Tiffany lived life with the enthusiasm of a hyperactive popcorn popper. A more animated, bubbly character I had never met. At first I thought she was just acting goofy for diversion, but soon I came to realize that she was being herself. I wondered how she could function that way. I actually thought she was a little too enthusiastic. Not my type, I decided.

But my type or not, I liked her and wanted to ask her out.

What was I thinking? She probably didn't take life seriously. What if she thought life was a joke? What if I discovered she was just a flake? Surely I couldn't marry such a person, so how could I ask her on a date? I knew she was temple worthy, since she went and did baptisms occasionally.

One day I was riding home from work with one of my coworkers.

"I don't usually give advice about dating," he said, "and I never liked setups, but would you be upset if I made a suggestion of who you could ask out?"

I didn't really want to hear his answer. One of the other girls from work was as quiet and shy as I could be, and I had been encouraged to ask *her* out before. And though she was a great girl, I wasn't really sure I wanted to. But now that he brought it up, I really had no choice but to answer.

"No, who are you thinking of?"

"You should ask out Tiffany."

I nearly choked on my own spit, and I'm sure my face reddened. But in a great effort to sound nonchalant, I replied, "Oh, really? Why do you say that?"

"I saw you guys talking at work the other day, and I thought, 'Ya know, those two would be good together.' "

Now I was sure I was blushing. "Hmm . . . I'll have to think about that."

Was I that obvious? I thought to myself. *Was it clear to everyone else that I had interest in her? Then again, if she already knew that I might be interested, and she hadn't yet turned cold on me, maybe she wouldn't be upset if I were to ask her out.* What was I to do?

Oh, good gracious, I told myself, *I'm acting like a high school kid. It's just a date, if I ask her. She may just say no anyway. At least that would save me the stress of worrying about it further. Of course, coming to work again would be awkward, but what if she said yes? Then work would be far more awkward.*

What am I thinking, we're nothing alike. She's way over-enthusiastic, and I'm . . . well, I'm kind of shy . . . usually. She's going into the medical field to become a nurse, and I'm studying to become a music teacher. Surely we had nothing in common . . . except maybe the gospel. But maybe she thinks the gospel is a joke . . . well, okay, so that's going a little far, but surely she won't be interested in me.

Finally I did the only sensible thing I could think of: I introduced her to my friend Donald and plotted to set him up on a date with her.

When that flopped, I knew I was cornered. I had a choice—forget the whole thing or ask her out myself. After another fit of anxiety, I chose the latter.

I got some friends together, and we decided to do a group date. One of the Michael McLean concerts was coming to town, so we planned to go to that. Deciding on a Michael McLean concert must have been an act of blindness on my part. I had long known that I was the only Deseret Book employee at the time that actually *liked* Michael McLean's music. It was a sort of taboo at our particular store to like his music, since it was such a big seller and always on the top ten lists. Don't ask me how that works out—I never could make sense of it. But she must have had great pity on me when I called because she agreed to go.

You know, girls often think guys are afraid to ask girls out because they are afraid they will be turned down. They think it's the fear of rejection that frightens them. But that wasn't the issue at all for me. It was the fear of success. If a girl said no, then my job was easy—forget the whole ordeal. But if she said yes, well, good grief, that meant I would have to go through the trauma of taking her on a *date*!

The date went well, to my surprise, and though I didn't say much, she talked enough for both of us. Of course, there were the occasional uncomfortable silences, but I knew that to be a normal part of dating—especially on first dates. When I dropped her off, I walked her to the door. We hugged, and I went back to the car, somehow feeling great. I hadn't made a terrible fool of myself, and she had enjoyed the date.

The drive home from a date was always an interesting experience for me. I found myself reviewing every conversation, analyzing every gesture, and trying to draw meaning out of every moment of the date. *What did she mean by what she said? Was that a way of trying to give me a clue that she's interested? Was it a clue that she's not interested? Maybe she mentioned that story about her dad to try to tell me that she wants to marry a guy like him—or maybe she was trying to warn me not to make the same mistake. How am I to know what it all means?*

I always did this after a date, and it was always agonizing. When I dropped a girl off, I felt great and considered the evening went well, and I was excited to tell people about it. But by the time I arrived home, I felt that she might as well have spit in my face and called me a world-class cheese ball. I had no desire to talk about the date with anyone. Hadn't I suffered enough already? But trying to avoid talking about a date when I got home was like diving into a piranha pool and trying not to get bit.

"So how did your date go?"

"Fine, Mom."

"Are you going to call her again soon?"

"Maybe, Dad."

"Well, you had a good time, didn't you?"

"Sure, Mom."

"Didn't *she* have a good time?"

"Sure, Dad."

Asking me about a date after the long, torturous, three-mile ride home was utterly useless. After a couple hours rolling around restlessly in bed, I would finally pass out from emotional trauma and sleep soundly the rest of the night. If you wanted the real story, you would have to wait about two weeks. By then I had a chance to come to terms with all that had happened.

And what *had* happened?

Nothing. It was a typical, harmless first date. It just took me two weeks to figure that out. After this recovery period, I would start thinking that maybe it hadn't gone as bad as I had imagined, and perhaps I ought to ask her out again. This is what happened with Tiffany. Unfortunately, she must not have recovered at all, because when I called again, she announced that she was moving to Logan.

nine

Blind Date

I have a suspicion that the only reason the blind date still exists is that for some few individuals, they actually work. The rest of us must suffer for the sake of the few.

Dad had a friend at work with a daughter my age, and somehow he managed to convince me to ask his daughter out. So he gave me her phone number, and after a couple weeks of putting it off, I finally called her. We talked for a bit, and I reluctantly asked her out. She agreed, and we scheduled a date for Friday night.

I have horrible orientation skills, so when I learned that this girl lived in Layton, I nearly panicked. I had never been to Layton, I had never known anyone from Layton, and I couldn't even guess which direction I would have to drive to get to Layton.

There is a tradition that men do not like to ask directions. I suppose this may be so for those who have some glimmer of confidence in their orientation skills. I had long since given up faith in mine. I would ask directions at a service station and follow them until I reached another service station. Then I would repeat the process until I was within a block or so of my destination.

Occasionally, however, I would get to a station where they didn't know the location I was looking for. In such circumstances, I would wander aimlessly through a city until I came across another service station—or, if there was no such station around, I might stop at a grocery store, restaurant, or business office to ask if anyone knew the way to my location. My family knew about my disorder, so they usually helped out. Dad offered to drive with me to the girl's house the night before the date so I would know how to get there.

When Friday night came, I was a bundle of nerves. This would be my first single date. I had only gone on group dates before. On group dates, you can always count on *someone* to carry on the conversation. With single dates, I knew I would have half the talking responsibility. I didn't even know this girl. What if we sat there in awkward silence for half the date?

Just to make sure I'd make it on time, and in case I got lost, I left forty-five minutes earlier than the expected travel time. As I left, I became conscious of everything. Had I put on enough deodorant? Too much? I didn't have a hair poking up, did I?

It was summer, and the air was hot and stuffy. This gave the inside of the truck a kind of muggy smell, and I wanted to impress my date. So I stopped at a service station and bought a car freshener. I got in the truck, popped it out of the bag, and hung it on the rear view mirror. I had never bought a car freshener before, and I was pleased with my choice—forest pine scent. That should give the car a nice fresh atmosphere. I also rolled the window down to let the old air out. Soon I realized the wind was scuffing up my hair, so I closed it.

After a time, I found my eyes watering with the intense scent of pine. Were car fresheners usually this powerful? I snatched the thing off the mirror and set it on the floor. That helped a little, but just to be sure, I opened the window a crack.

To my surprise, I arrived in good timing, giving me forty-five minutes to kill.

Perhaps if I had known Layton better, I could have window-shopped. But the risk of getting lost was too great, so I found a gas station, pulled around back, parked the truck, set my watch alarm to wake me, and tried to take a nap.

Next thing I knew, I opened my eyes and saw my date's dad

staring down at me through the window. "Getting a little sleep in, are we?"

"Uh, oh . . . hi! Yeah, I was just . . . I was a little tired."

He laughed and returned to his car. I could tell this was going to be a grand evening. After that I couldn't sleep.

By now, the car freshener was getting worse. I almost expected to see a green pine-scented mist emitting from the little tree. I fumbled through the truck till I found a plastic grocery bag to keep it in and stashed the chunk of aroma under the seat.

I showed up at Doreen's door at exactly 6:00 p.m. I didn't want to be early, in case her dad had told her about my gas station siesta, and I didn't want to be late lest she think I had overslept the said siesta. We left without going inside first, for which I was grateful. No need to meet her father.

The date started out all right—you know, the typical awkward silences followed by one of us (me, in this case) asking a dumb question like, "So where did you go to high school?"

I've only found one decent use for that question. You meet a girl and would like to know her age, so you ask, "Did you go to Cyprus High?"

"No, I went to Highland."

"Oh," you reply. "What year did you graduate?"

"1991."

Then you know she's too old. But on a first date, you thrive on small talk until you can grab onto something interesting to talk about.

Gratefully Doreen *was* close to my age and had already mentioned that she was going to school, so I asked, "So what are you studying?"

"Psychology."

Now I knew I was doomed. Not only was I on a blind single date, but I would be analyzed by an aspiring psychologist.

"What about you?"

"Music."

"And what would you like to do with your degree?"

"I don't know—maybe teach."

"How do you feel about teaching?"

"Uh, okay, I guess. I think it might be fun."

"And why is that?"

I know now why they call psychiatrists "shrinks." I felt very small. I felt like I should be laying on a big black couch, staring into a pastel light, as she at a desk with a clipboard, saying, "Interesting. Very interesting."

I wondered if I should start making up a bunch of horrible things that happened to me as a child that made me what I am today. Unfortunately nothing horrible ever happened to me as a kid. Maybe that's what made me such a dull date.

After another long silence, I noticed her eyes were starting to moisten. Had I said something to upset her? Had I offended her before our date had really began?

"Do you mind if I open the window?" she asked. "Your dad's air-freshener is burning my eyes."

I had been planning on taking her to the Lion House Pantry on Temple Square, but unfortunately I had not checked their hours ahead of time. The sign on the locked door announced that dinner was served from 5:00–7:00 p.m. It was 7:15. Short of walking over to the mall food court, the only other place to eat nearby was the Garden Restaurant at the top of the Joseph Smith Memorial building. Desperate to not look like a fool, I said, "Well, that's all right. I figured we could go up to the Garden Restaurant if this one was closed. Does that sound okay?"

"Whatever you'd like."

I was certain she was doing a psychoanalysis on my decision-making skills. I was determined not to fail. "Let's do it then."

I wonder if she saw my bug-eyed expression when I looked at the price of the menu items. "Get whatever you want," I assured her, hoping she didn't notice the crack in my voice.

It was a delicious meal, quite like home cooking, which made me wonder why we eat at such places. If we did make it at home, it would cost a tenth of the price and might even make for a more interesting date. But I guess that would require cooking skills. I decided I had best get some before going on another date.

After dinner, we had a tour of the Conference Center. Most of my early dates included a tour of the Conference Center. I probably could have provided the tour myself after a while, though that would have required a good deal more talking, which I was not very good at.

After the tour I asked her if she'd like to go see a laser show at Hansen Planetarium. I hadn't seen one in years, and I thought a date would be a good excuse to go.

"No," she replied, "I have lots of homework to do."

So I took her home. I walked her to the door, and after an awkward moment at the step, I turned and headed back for the car.

Thus ended my first single date. I guess it could have been worse. I could have fallen off the roof of the Conference Center or choked to death on a piece of chicken.

Driving home, I stopped at a service station and chucked the air freshener, riding the rest of the way with both windows down.

I took comfort in something someone once told me, which I found to be very true through the rest of my dating years. It is simply this: all first dates go badly. The first time you go on a date with a girl, with very few exceptions, the date will not go well.

Supposing that a first date is a forecast to the potential of the relationship is like assuming that seventh grade is a forecast of your academic future. Just imagine if that were the case. We would probably have Olympic spit-wad flings, and the Nobel Peace Prize would probably go to the one who had shut the largest number of annoying kids in their lockers. Likewise, if everyone assumed that a bad first date meant there was no chance for the relationship, most people would never get married.

That was the last I ever saw of Doreen. A couple days later, Dad came to me, a little confused. "Craig said Doreen told him my car freshener was too strong. I don't know what she's talking about. I don't have a car freshener."

ten

Hanging Out

Most of you have probably heard the talk by Elder Dallin H. Oaks about hanging out. Essentially he said that young adults need to do less hanging out and more dating. Since that time, a number of other talks, lectures, and firesides have been given on the same subject.

You are now at the most important decision-making stage of your life. The choices you make now will not only determine the course of your own life, but they will also determine who your children will be, where you will live, what kind of education you will pursue, and what your life's work will be. Obviously the most important decision is who you will marry. And right now, pursuing that goal should be your highest priority.

Elder Richard G. Scott taught: "If you are a young man of appropriate age and are not married, don't waste time in idle pursuits. Get on with life and focus on getting married. Don't just coast through this period of life. Young men, serve a worthy mission. Then make your highest priority finding a worthy, eternal companion."[1]

Most young adults are aware of the eternal importance of this decision, and understandably, they are greatly intimidated by it. That's normal. No matter how badly you want to meet someone and get married, the prospect of moving forward with the effort is both scary and dangerous. Perhaps that is why so many young adults get caught in the hanging-out trap. It's so much less stressful and much safer to simply hang out with a group of friends that includes guys and girls than to ask someone out. Why go through the trauma of asking someone out when you could just do the same activities with them by hanging out with your group of friends?

While this attitude is understandable, it's also counterproductive. It may increase your "popularity," but after high school, popularity isn't worth much. No wonder hanging out is especially tempting for the shy—it may be their first chance to feel accepted and included in a fun crowd. But you've got to remember that you're not in high school anymore, and your worth is not based on how many people are in your "group."

The truth is, there is nothing wrong with hanging out. In fact, it can be a great way to meet potential dating prospects. But the moment it becomes an end rather than a means, you run into trouble.

In the past few decades, the average marriage age for a young person has gone up while the number of children couples have has gone down. It used to be that a woman would get married around age twenty, a man at about age twenty-two. Now the average ages are about twenty-five and twenty-seven. While this may not seem like a big difference, think about how this is a national average. Overall, young adults are single for about five extra years. What are they doing during those years? For some, it's a time to get schooling done. For others it's an extension of high school, where social expectations are low and play opportunities are high.

Regardless of their reasoning, that's five extra years (more, for some) of unsuccessful dating. For this discussion, I'm defining successful dating as dating that leads to a permanent marriage relationship. So what is filling in that five-year gap? Either no dating, unsuccessful dating, or hanging out.

It used to be that there was no third alternative. But since hanging out feels somewhat fulfilling socially, it has become a substitution for real dating. It requires no commitment, and there is no need for painful breakups, rejection, or fear. But hanging out itself ultimately doesn't lead to marriage.

Have you ever noticed how the dynamics of a social situation change in a group versus one-on-one? While one-on-one time can be a little more intimidating to some, it is also so much more personal because it opens doors to communication in ways a group situation can never match.

If you aren't paired off, man and woman, then it's really not a date. Group dates are a great way to ease the pressure of a first date, and they can be a fun diversion. But for marriageable-age young adults, group dates should be the exception. If you *do* go on group dates, it should be with the goal to get one-on-one dates later, where you can really get to know each other.

If you are getting your ideals about dating from television and movies, it's time to change your perspective—completely. TV glamorizes dating as the highway to sex, and if that goes well for a time, perhaps we'll toss a marriage in. Even on the high-moral shows, where sex outside of marriage is discouraged, the wedding is portrayed as the glorious end.

Getting married may be your major goal, but if you forget that dating is a process of finding a *marriage partner*, and not just a wedding buddy, then you may find yourself married to someone you don't know.

You Don't Need Balloons to Ask Someone Out

When I was in high school, a girl asked me to dance with a box of donuts. A note inside said, "If you want to go to the dance with me, eat the donuts and return the box. If you don't want to go with me, eat the box and return the donuts."

I responded by giving her a two-liter pop bottle full of peanuts with my response rolled up inside one of them. There were a couple extras that said, "What's crackin'? Keep going!" and "Going nuts yet? Keep trying!"

Another time I asked a girl to a dance by making paper footprints that led from her porch, across the yard, and into a window well, where I placed a box of feet donuts and some cheesy message about dancing feet.

She responded with a 250-piece puzzle that I had to put together so I could flip it and read the message on the back.

Those kinds of experiences are fun, and they work great for high school, but they don't work for a genuine spouse search. You aren't trying to find a crafty asker; you're trying to find an eternal companion. What I'm saying is that a date doesn't have to be elaborate. It should be planned but flexible enough in case something interferes with the plan. Keep the plan simple: dinner and a movie, a visit to the zoo, or a walk in the park. In fact, more often than not, the simpler the date, the more you'll learn about each other. How much can you really learn about each other by renting laser tag equipment and reserving your ward gym with divider walls lined up like a maze?

If you think you must be overly creative in order to ask a girl out, then it's time to change your attitude. Plan something simple and fun, and you will learn enough about your date to get ideas for future dates.

Keeping it simple also makes it easier to go out more often. If every date is an expensive or elaborate event, the young man will be able to afford to go out only once a month. That won't get him married—unless of course he's dating someone out-of-state. And in that case, they will spend more time on the phone than anything else anyway.

USE CHIVALRY

Sometimes guys feel funny about taking their traditional expected initiatives such as asking girls out, opening doors for them, and offering to help them with their coat. They may fear coming across as chauvinistic or sexist. This may come as a surprise, but most girls don't usually see it that way. They are looking for a gentleman to marry, and they will be watching how you treat them. If you feel weird being the asker, just do it anyway. If you feel funny opening the door for them, try it anyway. Whether the girls act like they notice or not, they do.

Some guys think they have to do group dates in order to keep the dates appropriate and safe. This was certainly the case when you were a teenager, but it isn't anymore. Dallin H. Oaks made this clear when he said:

> For many years the Church has counseled young people not to date before age 16. Perhaps some young adults, especially men, have carried that wise counsel to excess and determined not to date before 26 or maybe even 36.
>
> Men, if you have returned from your mission and you are still following the boy-girl patterns you were counseled to follow when you were 15, it is time for you to grow up. Gather your courage and look for someone to pair off with. Start with a variety of dates with a variety of young women, and when that phase yields a good prospect, proceed to courtship. It's marriage time. That is what the Lord intends for His young adult sons and daughters. Men have the initiative, and you men should get on with it. If you don't know what a date is, perhaps this definition will help. I heard it from my 18-year-old granddaughter. A "date" must pass the test of three p's: (1) planned ahead, (2) paid for, and (3) paired off.[2]

When you make finding an eternal companion your number one priority, it becomes easier to step outside your comfort zone and ask someone out. It's harder than hanging out, but it leads to marriage. Hanging out doesn't. Elder Scott, speaking of this time of life when young adult men have returned from their missions, advised, "Get on with life. Try to identify as your first priority finding a worthy eternal companion and work at it. Don't just coast through this period of your life. It goes by too rapidly."[3]

GUYS REALLY DO WANT TO DATE

You would think that such direct language—telling young men to get out there and find someone—would upset young adult men who are already trying their best to do so. But the irony is that in my experience, this is the very counsel men thrive on. They *want* to be told that it's time to find someone. They *want* to be out there seeking their eternal companion. It's the world that applies so much pressure to wait. On nearly every side, they are told to focus on their education, to wait until after graduation to start dating, or to wait until they have a steady, fair-paying job. They are told that they are being naïve or selfish if they start dating seriously and that if they don't have a house, they are in no position to marry. Schools look down on marriage because they know it will put extra challenges on the students' efforts to complete their education. This pressure is real, even for the faithful who are strong in the Church. So it is a welcome relief when young men hear prophets telling them that it's not only okay to move forward but that it is a commandment and they should try to find a beautiful woman to marry.

President Harold B. Lee was very direct about this: "We are not doing our duty as holders of the priesthood when we go beyond the marriageable age and withhold ourselves from an honorable marriage to these lovely women."[4]

After sharing that quote in the priesthood session of general conference, President Thomas S. Monson said:

> I see lovely young ladies who desire to be married and to raise families, and yet their opportunities are limited because so many young men are postponing marriage. . . .
>
> Perhaps you are having a little too much fun being single, taking extravagant vacations, buying expensive cars and toys, and just generally enjoying the carefree life with your friends. I've encountered groups of you running around together, and I admit that I've wondered why you aren't out with the young ladies.
>
> Brethren, there is a point at which it's time to think seriously about marriage and to seek a companion with whom you want to spend eternity. If you choose wisely and if you are committed to the success of your marriage, there is nothing in this life which will bring you greater happiness.[5]

So if you find yourself getting caught in the hanging out trap, just decide right now that before the end of the day (yes, today), you will ask a girl out. Then do it!

If you're a young woman, and you don't feel comfortable about taking the initiative to ask a guy out, you may have to be more creative in your approach. If you have been hanging out for a long time with the same group and nothing has come of it, decide to stop hanging out. If anyone asks you why, just tell them that you're tired of the group activities *not* leading to real dating prospects. If the message gets around, it will remind the young men of their duties. Then use the extra time to find new venues that prove more useful. It may take trial and error to find the activities and groups that have young adults who are actually making the effort to date, but if it leads to eternal marriage, it will be worth it!

NOTES:

1. Richard G. Scott, "The Eternal Blessings of Marriage," *Ensign*, May 2011, 94–97.
2. Dallin H. Oaks, "Dating versus Hanging Out," *Ensign*, June 2006, 10.
3. Greg Hill, "Elder Richard G. Scott Answers Questions Asked by Young Single Adults," *LDS Church News*, October 19, 2009.
4. Harold B. Lee, "President Harold B. Lee's General Priesthood Address," *Ensign*, Jan. 1974, 100
5. Thomas S. Monson, "Priesthood Power," *Ensign*, May 2011, 66–69.

eleven

Just Do It

Giving dating advice is a funny thing. A person stumbles accidentally upon one incidental success, and suddenly he is regarded by his single friends as a professional relationship adviser. The truth is, you can only have true dating success once, because no matter how many times you fail, you can only marry once. Even divorce represents a failed relationship. Someone who is divorced and remarries five times cannot be said to have any true success unless it is on the fifth attempt. That's still only one success.

The wisest person learns from others and has no failures—but even that one success story lacks the lessons learned from dealing with failure. Take comfort in this fact: no matter how many times you fail, you only have to succeed once. If you persist in trying, then success is inevitable, because you will not give up until it comes.

After a few good failures, I began to realize that no matter how expert I became, I would never be fully qualified to give dating advice. Every girl was so unique and different from all the others. And in many ways, I was different than other guys. No one rule fits all cases.

It did help when I discovered that the dating game is a system established by our culture as the primary method for getting from singlehood to marriage. If you get to know the system well, you can become proficient at it. Practice can make perfect.

But no matter how talented you are at the dating game, it's your personality, your worthiness, and your attributes that make the biggest difference. You might know all the do's and don'ts of dating, and you might have the perfect plan, bank account, pickup lines, and all the etiquette that the books require but *still* be lacking in the most essential attributes.

Yet people aren't looking for a spouse who is a talented dater. They are looking for an eternal companion. Self-development is most important. Then you can concentrate on learning the system and getting good dating practice.

I also realized that the only way to learn to play the dating game is to date, so I decided that I would go on dates more regularly. I didn't tell myself I had to find a girlfriend right away. I just had to date. I was practicing and trying to master the dating game.

I thought dating so often would be difficult and terribly stressful, but it turned out to be only challenging the first couple of times. After that, I started feeling more comfortable. Dating was fun, and it actually felt like I was making some kind of progress toward marriage.

That period of my dating experience was incredibly enlightening. A seminary teacher once told me, "Go out with a hundred girls before you decide on a companion." While I would not put a number on how many people to date, I would recommend to guys that they ask out several girls before choosing one. Not only will this provide social practice, but it will expose you to young women's many qualities that will help you narrow down what you do and don't want in a wife. For girls, if they get a lot of opportunity to date, they might want to do the same. This is often difficult for girls, however, since they are not generally the askers, and guys should not expect them to be.

ASKING A GUY OUT

Having said that, I had a rule of thumb that seemed acceptable in most social circles about girls asking guys out: a girl can ask a guy out for a first date—that's fine. That's not being presumptuous at all. But if they end up going on the date, it then becomes the guy's responsibility to do the asking the next time. He cannot expect her to ask again, and she should not feel obligated to. If he doesn't ask her on a later date, it most likely means he's not interested. If he *is* interested, he needs to take the initiative to ask her out for a second date. After both have had a turn asking, then it is acceptable for either one to ask the other out. The guy should recognize that he has the primary responsibility to do the asking. But after they have been on a couple dates, the girl can ask the guy as much as she wants without having to worry about if she's being too forward.

That's not an established rule, but most guys accept that approach just fine. I suppose girls struggle with it more. Occasionally a girl will tell me about a guy she's interested in. After it's clear to me that she *really* wants this guy to ask her out but he's not taking the hint, I say, "Why don't you ask him out?"

Horrified, she usually says something like, "I can't ask him out! That's the guy's job! He would think I was being way too forward."

"I didn't say ask him to go steady. Just ask him on a simple date," I reply. "That's all you need to do to get him to notice you. If he can go, it will be up to him to do the asking next time. If he can't, at least he knows you would like to go out with him. Believe me, that knowledge makes it a great deal easier for him to ask you out later."

Usually, the girl will cower and refuse, saying she is too frightened. I then explain that it is perfectly normal to feel horrified beyond reason to ask someone out. Guys go through it every single time they ask a girl. The question is, is this guy worth a few moments of pure terror if it *just might* lead to something greater?

No matter what anyone says, most guys are absolutely worthless at taking hints. Chances are, no matter how many hints you've given him, he won't have a clue that you're interested in him if you don't ask him out. He's much more likely to ask someone out that he knows is interested in him than someone he thinks might not be interested. Asking him on a date is a clear message of *some* interest. Once you've asked him, whether or not he can go, he *will* notice you.

BUT WOULDN'T ASKING A GUY OUT SEEM TOO FORWARD?

Of course many girls then ask, "But won't I seem too forward? Won't that frighten him away?" First of all, away from what? If you're not already dating, you're not likely close enough to chase him away. You're more likely to run for cover than he is. You're the one with the feelings. If he has interest in you, he'll experience some anxiety, but it will be the anxiety of knowing what he must now do—ask you out. It's that wonderful, horrible, exciting anxiety that gets people out of their comfort zones and into each other's lives. If he doesn't have interest in you, then he never would have noticed you anyway (let alone asked you out) and in fact might start *becoming* interested in you from that time.

Besides, while you are sweating and freaking out, trying to take hints from every little move he makes or word he speaks, he's just living his life, clueless of the trauma you are experiencing. He's not in turmoil. You are. You probably have enough emotional energy built up to split an atom. He's probably thinking about his next meal. While you stress about whether he will ever ask you out, he's not even thinking about it at all. Until you *place* the ball in his hands, he will probably never have a clue that there is a ball. When you ask him out—no matter the response—he will realize there might be another option other than casual acquaintance with you. And he *will* think about it.

So what kind of date do you ask him on? And how do you go about doing it?

When you ask him out, be sure to use the word *date*. If you don't say the word *date*, he will probably not know that's what it is, and if he is as clueless as some guys are, he may bring friends—or even a date. (Ugh! Can you imagine?!)

Call it a date, double-date, group-date, or even friend-date if you must, but use the word *date*. Girls understand the essentials of communication, but they can also think that hints, clues, and signs are communication. That may be so with other girls, but it is *not* so with guys. When you're speaking to guys, you need to speak specifically;

otherwise, you have not communicated with him.

How do you avoid seeming desperate or too forward? Here is a simple test: if you find it easy to ask guys out, you need to be careful about seeming too desperate or too forward. Your personality will automatically radiate enough interest to give him the hint.

If, on the other hand, it uses up all your emotional energy and a disproportional amount of courage to ask the guy out, don't worry about it at all. Your personality cannot and will not come across as too forward. Even when feel like you are desperate and being a silly lovesick fool, if it takes that much courage to ask a guy out, then chances are you'll never come across as too forward to any guy.

Don't hide from him after you've asked him out, no matter how good or bad things went. If you are the one with all the feelings, then the situation is only awkward for you. To him, it's all very flattering and interesting. It only gets awkward for him if you nag him about the date too much after you've already asked.

I know a good number of guys who married a girl who asked them out for the first date. In most cases, it was the fact that she asked him that gave him the hint or courage to ask her out the next time. Remember, just because you shouldn't feel the obligation to ask a guy out doesn't mean you can't do it. Just because it really is the guy's responsibility to ask doesn't mean your banned from the possibility.

BUT WE'RE *SUCH* GOOD FRIENDS!

One of the fears I experienced while I was dating, and which you may be now experiencing, is this: *If I ask this girl out, it may spoil our friendship. I would hate to do that. I really like how we are such good friends, and if I ask her out, it might become awkward, and things will never be the same.*

To that I say, forget it. It's a valid concern, but it's useless. Think about it. If you end up marrying someone else, your friendship with that girl will become virtually obsolete. If she marries someone else, your friendship will become obsolete.

What do I mean by obsolete? When you get married, you and

your spouse are your primary social life. And while you may occasionally hang out with people of your own gender, it would be inappropriate to hang out with people of the opposite gender. So old friends of the opposite gender become acquaintances with whom you have very limited contact. Besides, you or your friend will most likely move away, which will probably entirely break all contact. While you still consider each other a friend, there will be no real communication, so your friendship becomes obsolete.

So this friend you have now may be a *good* friend, but you don't want to ruin it and make it awkward by asking her out. So you remain a bachelor and she a bachelorette, forever, and you remain forever buddies—well, is that *really* how you want to be? Unmarried for life? If you don't want to remain a bachelor forever, you'll need to start dating someone eventually. So, for heaven's sake, just ask her out! You really can't lose.

And if you really want to keep this close friendship with someone of the opposite sex, your best chance is to ask them out. If you marry, it will last forever. If you don't marry, it will end fairly soon. So why put it off and take the chance that she might marry someone else? Why not ask her out now? If it works, you're friendship will only get stronger, and you'll never regret your decision.

twelve

Catching Someone's Eye Without Blinding Them

One of the biggest challenges during the dating years is trying to get a particular someone's attention without scaring the daylights out of them. Whether they are just too clueless to notice your hints, or you are too clueless to properly drop hints, or every time you enter the room, she bolts out the back door, the effort to get someone's attention can be exasperating.

Obviously it's going to be a little different for men than it is for women—especially since men are traditionally supposed ask the woman out. But that doesn't mean girls have to sit and wait. In fact, because girls have a more reactive role in this arena, they need to be even more creative and proactive in being noticed.

Some guys feel they want to know a girl before asking her out. If you are such a guy, you're also going to need to learn how to get a girl's attention.

So whether you are a guy or a girl, if you have found someone to target, how do you go about getting his or her attention and gently letting that person know you are interested without scaring him or her away?

YOUR MIND-SET
The first thing you will want to do is change your dating mind-set—a

date is casual and noncommittal. If your mind-set is that dating is informal, you will portray that to others. Set your goal on either getting guys to ask you out, or, if you're a guy, getting girls comfortable with the idea of you asking them out.

YOUR LOCATION

Find out enough about the person to know where she goes and what she does. Obviously you don't want to stalk her, but find out what classes she's taking or where she likes to hang out. Then go there. Be there when she shows up. If you want her to notice you, you'll have to be where she is. No matter how much you notice her at a distance, she will not notice you unless you are where she'll see you. This goes for girls and guys.

HOW TO FLIRT APPROPRIATELY

Flirting is not flaunting yourself—it's more like garnishing your personality. But it must be specialized for the person you want to attract. If you flirt with everyone, you lose the power. You may even come across to others as shallow or desperate. But done carefully and appropriately, flirting can be an effective tool to give that certain someone a nudge that you are here.

The world's concept of flirting can be a little twisted and often focuses too much on the sexual side of your nature. Don't get your ideas from movies and books. While those methods may work if you're targeting someone with low standards, they can likely scare away a worthy, active member of the Church. But this doesn't mean flirting is wrong or even unwise. It just means flirting must be done appropriately and tastefully if you want to get your target's attention without scaring him away. Remember, the secret isn't to convince your target that he likes you; it's to gently let him know you're interested in dating.

Be Clean and Well Groomed

It doesn't take much effort to be well groomed. Comb your hair, brush your teeth, shower daily, and use deodorant. If you're a guy, shave and keep your hair moderately trimmed. Believe it or not, most girls like that; they generally find a clean, well-groomed guy more attractive than a scruffy, long-haired guy. Girls, you may want to try some makeup, but don't overdo it. Just use enough to complement your features. The secret is to use just enough that a guy won't know you have it on.

Wear clothes that are comfortable and modest. Revealing attire will attract the wrong people. Besides, you want them to be attracted to *you*, not just your body. How do you know if clothes are modest? Very simply, if clothes would cover temple garments and are not skin tight or transparent, they are sufficiently modest. Believe it or not, to good people, modesty is more attractive. This is because good people know that to be respected is greater than to be loved.

Don't Use Conversation Starters—Just Start a Conversation

When you first approach your target, you will probably be scared to death and unsure how to break the ice. If you approach with the mind-set of casual friendship, it will make things a lot easier for both of you. Be casual and fun, and you really can't lose.

Using a pickup line is an instant way of saying, "I'm the biggest cheeseball on the planet, and I like you!" Rather than trying to be witty or seductive, act comfortable. Don't plan some fancy or clever conversation starter, just start a normal, everyday conversation. It could be as simple as asking if the person knows the time or commenting on the weather. The idea is to get him talking to you. Don't break out the moves or try to rush into anything before you get a casual conversation started.

It may sometimes be okay to use humor to start a conversation, but don't try to be clever about it. If you begin with a tease, make sure it's a non-sarcastic, impersonal tease that doesn't put any pressure on him or make the situation awkward.

Be Confident

You may not feel confident when you are in the presence of someone you have your eye on, but acting in confidence will bring out the best in your personality. But don't confuse confidence with conceit or cockiness. Both conceit and cockiness come across as insecure and unattractive. Confidence means you act comfortable in her presence. You talk to your target as you would an old friend.

Maintain Eye Contact

This is probably the most important trick to good flirting. Eyes communicate even more powerfully than the mouth. Maintaining good eye contact tells your target that you are interested in what she is saying. During a brief silence, prolonged eye contact might tell the person that you are interested in *her*. Of course, this doesn't mean staring her down. Eye contact that is too persistent may make you seem desperate or overbearing. Look away just often enough to keep the situation from becoming awkward, but good eye contact will send a powerful message of openness and interest. As a note, never look at other parts of a person's body besides the head. Not only is it totally inappropriate to "check them out," but it suggests that you are not very disciplined or respectable. Whether that was the intent or not, that may be the message she receives.

Smile a Lot

Smiles are the easiest way for you to send your target a strong positive message. Your smile will *always* make you look more attractive, no matter how crooked and yellow your teeth are. If your smile is sincere, it will send your target the message that you like being in his presence. Next to eye contact, smiles are probably your biggest flirting tool. Also, if you accidentally get caught staring, don't look away, just smile!

Show Kindness

It helps to remember that not only is your target hoping to marry someone who is charming and attractive, but most of all she wants someone who is good and worthy. Since this trick is an attribute, it can't be faked. It has to be developed and nurtured, so make sure you practice this attribute while flirting. Genuine kindness always, *always* leaves a positive impression. Offer kind gestures, such as giving them a hand with something or offering them a piece of gum or candy. Don't be forceful about it, and don't turn down any kindness she offers you. Be gracious by saying, "thank you," and "you're welcome." These are not just kind words—symbols of the deeper attributes of kindness, graciousness, and understanding.

Have Close Proximity and Physical Touch

Of all of the tricks mentioned in this chapter, be most careful with this one. It's a powerful tool, so it must be used sparingly and appropriately, or it could blow your chances. It can cause the most intense reaction, for good or bad, so be wise in how you use it, especially if you don't know the person well.

Remember in grade school how they used to talk about your "personal bubble"? That wasn't just an elementary thing. There is a socially established rule of physical proximity that we know as personal space. The distance varies through different cultures in the world, but the generally accepted distance for the average person in American culture is eighteen inches. That means when two people are talking, it is considered invasive to get closer than eighteen inches. The *average* distance is more like thirty inches.

When you're trying to flirt, and it seems to be going well, close the distance between you a bit. If you are used to standing three feet from people as you talk to them, try closing the distance with your target to two feet. Don't cross the eighteen-inch line, or the other person may freak out, but get closer to it. This will intensify the power of your eye contact and give him the sense that you enjoy being close to him. If he backs off when you get closer, you back off too. The last thing you want to do is make your target uncomfortable.

If the situation is appropriate, briefly touch him on the arm. Not often or regularly, but just once, for a moment. The arm is generally safe if it is done at the right moment. You can also brush lightly past him as you pass by, but make sure you only brush the shoulder or arm.

With physical touch, you don't want to come across as clingy or leechy. Guys must be especially careful not to come across as "all hands." That can be a big turnoff for girls. If you are on a date, you can try touching your date's hand a little too, if the situation is appropriate.

Never ever touch an inappropriate part of the body for any reason whatsoever.

The point of physical touch and close proximity in flirting is not to get a rush but to gently communicate your interest.

Have Substance

Make sure that in your flirting, you bring up topics that make it clear to your target that you have substance. You can tease and joke, but if your target doesn't learn some of the deeper aspects of your personality, she may think you are flaky and lose interest. Talk about your interests, hopes, and dreams. Even better, have her talk about her interests, hopes, and dreams. Encourage her in the things that matter most to her. If you can, bring up spiritual topics that will allow you to share your feelings about the gospel. When your target sees beyond the surface of your personality, she will feel closer to you—whether she takes interest in you or not. Sharing your substance with your target will build or strengthen your friendship, which gives you the best chance possible to encourage a deeper relationship.

This tip is especially important when your target is a strong, active member of the Church. She's looking for an eternal companion—an eternal, trusted, respectable friend. All the playful flirting in the world will not win her over if she can't sense your deeper personality.

Be Optimistic

Few things can break your chances with someone as fast as negative comments. Obviously you don't need to be a Pollyanna, but don't be a Scrooge either. The more positive you are in your comments and conversation, the more positive an impression you will make on your target. Don't be fake, but keep on the bright side as much as possible. People like being with optimists, and your target is no exception.

Show Wise and Tasteful Use of Non-Sarcastic Humor

There's a reason I don't just call this tip "Humor." So much of modern humor is sarcastic, demeaning, inappropriate, or rude—it would be better to never attempt to be funny than to fall into that trap. The last thing you want to do is come across as inconsiderate or rude.

Having said that, one of the ways to leave a great impression is getting your target to laugh. It is difficult to explain how to do this, since every situation provides a completely different opportunity for humor, but if you watch for simple ironies and decorate them with a touch of obvious exaggeration or animation, you can make even the stiffest situation funny.

Just remember to never seek a laugh at the expense of another person. Because humor can be so easily misunderstood or misinterpreted, only use it if you know your target well enough to know what she would find funny. Humor takes a lot of confidence and a little practice, so if you try something out and it bombs, best just put it away for when you know your target better. With time, she'll recognize your style of humor and know when you're joking.

Tease Gently and Appropriately

This approach is similar to humor, but with teasing you have to be even more careful. If you don't know how to tease in a kind, fun way, don't try it. You may burn all bridges of opportunity. The object of teasing is not to demean, put down, or belittle in any way. It is to find fun and light methods of complimenting your target in ways that gives the impression you like your target without making him feel awkward. Careful teasing also has a way of singling your target out, which can be a good way to draw attention to the fact that he's been on your mind. But again, if you don't know how to tease in a way that doesn't belittle, or you're not sure how your target would react to your teasing, don't try it.

Generally speaking, guys like teasing more than girls do. So if you're a guy, be extra careful with teasing. If you're a girl, do it more, since he'll feel like you are singling him out, which he will like. Either way, be sensitive and use teasing sparingly.

Give Genuine Compliments

Here's a tip you can use liberally without the fear of offending. Don't shower your target with shallow accolades as that will seem insincere. Instead look for opportunities to genuinely compliment her. If you are going to compliment her looks, do it in a general way. The more specific you are about complimenting her looks, the more risk you take. Saying something like, "You look great!" is almost always safe. If you must be specific, focus on the head, such as hair or eyes. You could even say something like, "Your outfit really brings out the color in your eyes." It might also be okay to say, "I really like your outfit." But if you get too specific, it may make her feel strange, like you're checking out her body. Incidentally, avoid tagging the word, "today," at the end of your compliment, such as, "you look great today," as she may read it as, "You don't usually look great, but today you do!"

The best way to be safe with compliments is to focus on other aspects of the person, such as attributes, talents, services, or skills. If you know your target's interests, compliment her on the things she has accomplished in those fields. Whether your target takes the compliment graciously or not, it will still make her feel good. By focusing compliments on the more meaningful parts of her personality, you send the message that she is a great person worth knowing. It also may help her find that she likes being around you, because of the way you make her feel.

If your target closes up or becomes uncomfortable every time you pay a compliment, then cut back a bit and keep your compliments unspecific.

The key to compliments is to keep them sincere—*always* sincere.

Show Appropriate and Careful Emphasis on Your Femininity or Masculinity

Be careful about this one, because you do not want to give your target the wrong idea or place too much emphasis on the physical aspect of your interest. But the key you have for getting your target's attention is your gender. Emphasizing your feminine or masculine nature can be very attractive to your target, and it also sends a subconscious message to your target that you know your role.

As much as society has done to confuse gender roles, we all still have instincts toward those parts of our nature that set clear gender duties, and our biology and spirituality still consider those roles part of our very being.

So what does that have to do with flirting? Consider the most basic general tendencies of men and women, and use them subtly in your mannerisms while talking to your target.

If you are a man, be assertive, protective, confident, and strong. Don't be overbearing or boastful, but be kind, decisive, and serviceable. Subtly emphasize your stature—not in an intimidating way, but in a way that makes you look like the kind of guy that could keep a girl safe and ready to help whenever you get the chance.

If you are a woman, be kind, gentle, and nurturing. Don't act submissive or fearful, but be loving, compassionate, and inquisitive. Keep a good posture, and find ways to draw attention to your hair. Guys go gaga for a girl's hair. It's one of the physical features that you can draw attention to without promoting inappropriate thoughts in him. Swoosh it around occasionally or play with it with your fingers.

There is pressure in the world to forget gender roles and become equal in every aspect, but in the gospel we know that God has given us clearly defined roles. By considering our natural tendencies within those roles, and using mannerisms that emphasize your recognition of your duties within those roles, you'll attract others who feel that those roles and duties are important.

SOME THINGS TO KEEP IN MIND WHEN FLIRTING

Statistically speaking, people generally end up with a spouse who is approximately of their same attractiveness level. While this is not always true, it generally works out that way, and there are some psychological reasons for this. For one, people are generally intimidated by partners who are more attractive than they are and are also more prone to jealousy or suspicion of their partner. They may also occasionally get overly self-conscious about their partner's interest in them. When they assume that they are not attractive to their partner, they may become either elusive or temperamental.

Again, this is not always the case. There are plenty of couples where one of the spouses is far more attractive than the other, but it helps to keep this possible issue in mind while considering someone as a target.

If you're going to consider this, however, you should also keep in mind that a girl tends to think of herself as less attractive than she really is, while a guy tends to assume that he is more attractive than he really is. If you're a girl, and you know you have a tendency to doubt your beauty, don't be afraid to target guys who are a little more attractive. If you're a guy who tends to target the most attractive girls, consider toning it down a bit and looking for a girl whose beauty will grow on you. It may save you a lot of heartache and rejection.

In doing this, make sure you're not setting your sights out for someone based completely on their looks. Attractiveness helps, and it ought to play a small factor, but ultimately it's not an enduring part of a lasting relationship. All of us who live to be old will lose our physical attractiveness eventually, so find someone who has the worthiness, character, and attributes that will make her the best marriage partner possible. Broaden your horizon a little bit to see if there are some great prospects you've been overlooking.

Also, when flirting, remember you don't want to be a different person around your target than you are with everyone else. Don't act warm and friendly to your target but cold and thoughtless to everyone else. At the same time, don't flirt with everyone around, because this will make you look desperate. The simple secret is to use kindness, optimism, and genuineness with everyone, and reserve close proximity, openness, teasing, touch, and lingered eye contact (the things you wouldn't do around a married person) for your target. Smiles, of course, can go for both also, but you'll just want to use them more often with your target.

~~~~~

thirteen

For Loved Ones Who
Want to Help

Y ou've probably all heard the quote that claims that any man
who reaches the age of twenty-five without being married is a
menace to society. I don't know if that quote came from Brigham
Young, Steve Young, or Steve Martin, but it's not true.

So what if you're a parent, sibling, or friend who wants to see
your loved ones experience the joys of marriage, but you can see that
so far, they are not having success? Do you start setting them up with
people? Do you give them advice? You see that they want to marry,
so what can you do to help?

It's a sticky issue, but a real one. The first answer is in the scriptures:

> And again, the angel said: Behold, the Lord hath heard the
> prayers of his people, and also the prayers of his servant, Alma, who is
> thy father; for he has prayed with much faith concerning thee . . . for
> this purpose have I come . . . that the prayers of his servants might
> be answered according to their faith.
>
> And he caused that the priests should assemble themselves
> together; and they began to fast, and to pray to the Lord their
> God. . . .
>
> And it came to pass after they had fasted and prayed for the
> space of two days and two nights, the limbs of Alma received their
> strength . . . (Alma 27:14, 22, 23)

There you have it. You can pray. It may seem simplistic, and it may seem futile, but remember that God has more influence on the world than all other beings combined, and sometimes it takes more than just the faith of the individual. Your faith has more power than you know. The nice thing about prayer is that you don't have to worry about stepping out of your bounds. Offering advice, setting up, and dropping hints all have the place can be easily abused. But you're always safe with prayer, since it's never inappropriate or over-bearing. You can ask Father in Heaven to help your loved one find someone wonderful to marry, and He acts on that request in His own time and way. Remember that He loves your loved one even more than you do.

GIVING ADVICE

If you are asked for advice, be gentle how you administer it. Remember, your loved ones are coming to you for advice—they are placing *great* trust in whatever you say. If you spill out whatever thoughts first come to your head, you may lead them into trouble. Try to learn his situation, and based on your knowledge of the person, give advice that is appropriate and safe. You may want to offer a prayer in your heart for guidance. Don't be afraid of giving advice—he's smart enough to weigh your words against his own judgment—but give it gently.

If you have never been married, it may be helpful to remember that you haven't experienced success yourself, so your advice must be taken with that in mind. You may even want to remind your loved one of that, just to ensure that he doesn't take your advice as the great answer to all dating problems.

If you are married, try hard to remember your thoughts and feelings from your own dating years. It seems so simple now. *But it didn't seem simple at the time!* And admit it, if your spouse died and you were back in the "game," it still wouldn't be simple now either. Besides, it's always easy to see how the pieces came together through introspection, but you can't see the future, so the pieces do not fall in place easily.

Also remember, every person on earth is a unique individual, and there is no advice (other than to pray) that works for every person. Think about it: this person is an eternal being who has always existed and always will exist. He is now in a mortal state where it is easiest to make mistakes, where he has a veil of forgetfulness over his mind, and where pain, suffering, and trials are inevitable. If he has done things right, he will spend the rest of eternity bound to another person, and every decision made for the rest of his existence will be made *with* that person. Other than God Himself, those two people will have a greater influence on each other than anyone else in the universe.

Why should we keep this in mind when asked for dating advice? Simply because the person your loved one marries will ultimately determine who he is for the rest of eternity. If he's momentarily vulnerable, he may take your advice whether it's wise or not. Would you risk flippant and carelessly dealt advice on such odds? One way this happens is when someone is trying to offer encouragement when the person is feeling down or worried. If it is an inappropriate or abusive relationship and you don't know it, then giving advice that saves the relationship may be the worst thing you can do.

I like to think of giving dating advice as giving out a prescription. How frightening would it be if you went to the doctor for a bad stomachache and before even examining your symptoms or asking about your allergies or condition, he prescribed antibiotics. What if your problem was appendicitis? Not only will the antibiotics do nothing, but the doctor may be the cause of death, since he treated the wrong problem.

If someone asks you for advice, ask for symptoms. What kinds of efforts is he presently making? How have they worked out so far? What has worked and what hasn't? What is the present condition of the relationship? What's the person like? What are the motives of both parties? Chances are, your loved one will discover what prescription he needs just by telling you his symptoms.

In short, follow the Spirit and do more listening than advising. If you don't know what to tell your loved one, encourage him to pray and express confidence in his ability to make the right decision. Remember that God loves him more than you do and will guide him if he humbly seeks God's direction.

ASKING FOR ADVICE

If you're seeking advice, recognize first Heavenly Father is the best to advise you. Most often the next in line is your parents, then your Church leaders, and finally your friends and other loved ones. Some people are too shy to go to Church leaders about something like dating advice, so it is okay to go to friends. Just make sure your friends are trustworthy. If your friend has messed up his own life, he has no good advice to give you. Even if he says, "This is what I should have done . . ." he may just as likely be wrong.

Go to someone you know cares about you. Go to someone you trust, and most of all, go to someone who has what you want! It can be a roommate who is dating someone steadily or someone who has a spouse and children—like you want. Just make sure this someone makes it easier for you to live the gospel of Jesus Christ. The moment he encourages you to act against the commandments or let your standards down, you can be absolutely certain that his advice is trash, no matter how convincing it may seem in the moment. If you are ever encouraged to act against the law of chastity, then reject the advice completely, and don't seek or take advice from that person.

When you ask the trusted friend for advice, listen carefully to what he says. His advice may or may not be what you need—you need to judge that for yourself, but think carefully on what your friend says.

If you have been through driver's ed, you may remember the importance of checking blind spots. A blind spot is an area around your car that you cannot see through the regular instruments designed for giving the fullest vision possible. Rearview and side mirrors provide a good perspective of most of the area around your vehicle, but no matter how much coverage those instruments provide, some areas are simply not visible. Every car has blind spots, but each vehicle has various sizes of blind spots in different parts of the driver's peripheral vision. Car accidents are often the result of the driver not checking a blind spot.

No matter how good a person you are, you are not perfect. You have things about your personality and mannerisms that you can't see. You have blind spots. A car is not defective because it has blind spots, and neither are you. You have parts of your personality and mannerisms that you cannot see that may turn others off from wanting to date you. Those spots are normal and mortal. Chances are, your friends and loved ones can see those spots. You may want to ask them about them. Be willing to take whatever painful revelations they give. If they say, "It would probably help if you spent a little more time combing your hair," don't outright reject their comment as a jerky thing to say. Consider it, and try to fix it. If it makes the difference, it will be worth whatever embarrassment the revelation may give you.

SETTING UP

Everyone has different feelings about setups. One person might beg people to set him up with their friends while another would rather gag on a hot coal than be set up with someone he doesn't know.

Before you consider setting someone up, do two things: find out both people's feelings about being set up, and find out HOW they would like to be set up. If either person doesn't like being set up, then don't try it. If they do, ask them for their preferred method of being set up.

For example, when I was dating, some people would set me up with a cousin or friend by giving me her number and telling me to call. They would say something like, "I'll let her know you're going to call."

I hated that. Oh, how I hated that. For some people, that method worked great, since it allowed them to plan what kind of date and how much money to spend. But for me, it was awful.

My preferred method was for the setter-upper to talk to the girl and arrange a double date. Then the setter-upper would plan the place, time, and activity and have me meet them there at the appointed time. Then when I arrived, they could introduce me to my date and we'd have a great time together—all four of us. I didn't like setups at all unless the setter-upper used this method.

Not to say my way works best, because some people don't like my way. My point is ask the individual you want to set up what *his* preferred method is. If his method puts more responsibility on you than you're comfortable with, then don't set him up. If it's manageable, go ahead and do it.

After the date, please—*please*—don't nag either of the two. Of course you want to know if they are going to go out again. Of course you hope things work out between them, and you would *love* to see them get together, but there's something you have to remember: it's none of your business. None at all.

Obviously if they bring it up, you can gently ask about it, and offer general encouragement if they are willing to talk more about it, but it is not your place to apply any pressure for them to move forward. Remember, it's none of your business. You did your part—and it was a major part—but the moment that first date is done, you are out of the picture unless they come to you about it. And if they do, remember to deal out advice cautiously.

86

fourteen

~~~

True Love

Love, *true* love, is not something we "fall" into. It is not acciden-
tal. To suggest this demeans the depth and power of true love.
True love involves choice—it involves a great deal of agency and a
great deal of action. We commonly mistake infatuation for love.

In a classic talk about agency in love and marriage, Lynn G.
Robbins of the Seventy said:

> For some people, falling in love is a magical encounter,
> something that seems to happen at first sight. For others, it is
> a growing affinity and attraction toward another, like budding
> blossoms that flower into a beautiful bouquet. Though the first
> type of love may also bloom like the second, it is often merely
> glandular, a cotton candy kind of love that has no substance.
> While it may begin with warm cuddles in moonlit glades, it can
> soon grow cold as honeymoon memories fade and familiarity
> turns to faultfinding.[1]

THE HEART LEADS THE WAY

Thinking back on my earliest crushes, I can't help acknowledging
the simplicity of them. In those earliest days, I had no real concept
of sexual interest. The very thought of such was mortifying to me.
Without doubt, I was very physically attracted to certain girls, but at

that time, my deepest, most secret desire was simply to spend time with the girl. To be around her.

Even the thought of holding a girl's hand was frightening to me. It's not that I didn't want to hold hands, but that thought was intimidating enough to scare me away from a girl entirely. In my earliest years, my only interest was seeing the girl—even at a distance. Then, as I approached my mid-teens, being with a girl was as great a thing as anything I could imagine.

Once I had been on a few dates with various girls, I thought it would be fun to pair off, just me and the girl. Then we could talk and converse alone—openly, honestly, and completely. This sounded more exciting and alluring than anything else I could imagine.

After I'd been home from my mission for some time and had been given many opportunities to pair off with a girl to converse alone, I thought the coolest thing would be to date each other exclusively—to be officially boyfriend and girlfriend.

It didn't take me long in this process to realize that one ultimate "goal" eventually leads on to another. At first it was to see the girl. Then it was to spend time in her presence. Then pairing off and so on. It occurred to me that relationships guide feelings.

I remember feeling completely alien to the idea of having a girlfriend and especially to the idea of having a *wife*. How could *I* get married? It's not that I didn't want to, it was just that I felt so inadequate, so incapable, of all the preliminary requirements. It was tempting to think it would be impossible for me to ever have the opportunity.

As I dated more, and as I had more experiences with relationships, I realized that relationships perpetuate *themselves*. Our natural, even unpracticed instincts urge us from one step on to the next. They give us just enough foresight to predict what might just be coming up next and just enough comfort and drive to move us on to the next step.

That's why even the shyest people get married. That's why even the most awkward, backward individuals can find themselves forming eternal relationships. It's more than just their own willpower at work. Their instincts carry them one step at a time, and before they know it, they're married with children. This is also why we have to be so careful and make sure to keep the law of chastity with exactness—both the spirit and letter of the law. The body will urge you on to the next step, making what once seemed terrifying now seem normal and natural.

Once I realized this, it became much easier to concentrate on where I was and what I was doing. On a date, I had to only concentrate on what was to happen on that one date.

So while on a first date, I never had to stress out about how to propose to this person someday. I didn't have to think about marriage. I didn't have to stress about eventually having to combine bank accounts or balance a checkbook with this person. Sure, I still needed to watch for financial red flags, but I didn't have to worry about planning a retirement fund with this person. I didn't have to freak out about intimacy—that was a step far beyond what was expected of me now. For the early dates with a girl, I didn't even have to stress out about holding hands or kissing. Those things were for later, and I couldn't expect to be prepared for them before my natural inclinations drove me in that direction.

BE CAREFUL WITH THE PHYSICAL

This principle also illustrates why a couple must be so careful about physical intimacy from the very start of their relationship. Just as one commitment, such as a date, leads to another, such as a courtship, so one physical act, such as hand holding, can lead to another, such as kissing. While the idea of kissing a person may scare the socks off you now, in time it will not. In time you will want it more than almost anything. That's human nature. That's our biological instinct.

Lowell Bennion illustrated this principle when he said:

> Once a couple begins to share affection in a physical way, this activity tends to become the focus of interest. Often such a couple ceases to explore the other significant dimensions of personality: mind, character, maturity, religious faith, moral values, and goals.
>
> Affection should grow out of genuine friendship and brotherly

love, not precede them, if one wishes to be sure of having real and lasting love in marriage. Kissing for the sake of kissing invites more affection, and many fine young people become more deeply involved than they actually wish to be.[2]

We must decide now, even before we begin dating, what we will and will not do. We must decide before the first date that we will never break the law of chastity under any circumstances. We must decide that we will only date those who share that standard.

We can also use this principle to set our time frames. If your date wants to kiss you on your first date, and you've decided that you will not kiss until you're exclusive, you won't have to ask yourself what to do when the opportunity comes. You'll already know.

M. Gawain Wells said:

> Some people also use physical affection as a measure of the progress of the relationship—and that's a false and irrelevant measurement. A girl might think, "If he holds my hand, it means he likes me." Or, "If he puts his arm around me, that means he likes me more." But those gestures might mean nothing of the sort. In fact, a too-quick development of such gestures may lead to inappropriate expressions of affection and thus damage a healthy relationship. If a courtship is based largely on physical affection, you probably need to evaluate its stability.[3]

Relationships are such that neither partner should ever have to do something they don't feel comfortable doing. If the relationship has potential to eventually blossom into marriage, then every natural inclination will certainly come with time. There's no need to rush any of it.

One healthy approach is to look at the relationship from all sides.

Let's say you have been dating someone for two months, and you are beginning to feel like you want to date exclusively. Look at all the sides of the relationship. How is the physical attraction? How does the physical progress compare with the emotional progress? What about the intellectual progress? The spiritual? What about communication progress? This is a good time to see if anything is out of balance. Are there a lot of physical expressions but little spiritual connection?

If so, perhaps you need more time to develop those things that are lacking. If with more time, you find that this unbalance is a fundamental difference that could cause later problems, this may be a good sign that it's time to end the relationship. On the other hand, if there *is* balance, move on.

COME UP WITH SOME PERSONAL GUIDELINES

In my early dating, I didn't think about this progress in such detail, but I did have a few guidelines for myself.

As for the physical side, I was scared to death of the idea of kissing, though I had no doubt it would be pleasurable. I decided that kissing was at a very high physical level of progression in a relationship, and I would not participate in it until I had reached equally high levels of spiritual and emotional progress with this person. I thought of Spencer W. Kimball's words: "Kissing has . . . degenerated to develop and express lust instead of affection, honor, and admiration. To kiss in casual dating is asking for trouble. What do kisses mean when given out like pretzels and robbed of sacredness?"4

I didn't want to make that mistake, so I made a rule for myself about kissing. Specifically, I decided I would not kiss a girl unless I knew I loved her. It was not to be a sign of mere infatuation or physical attraction. To me, a kiss was a physical way of saying, "I love you." That also implied that I didn't need to kiss her until I had at least told her that I loved her, and she felt the same.

I also decided I would not allow myself to fall in love with someone who was not a faithful member of the Church in good standing. She had to be worthy of a temple recommend. If she was temple worthy, and I was in love with her, and she with me, a kiss would be permissible—an appropriate, premarital kiss, that is! In my book, an appropriate premarital kiss meant mouths closed.

KISSING A FORM OF COMMUNICATION?

After I decided this, it was easy to avoid the stress of wondering whether or not to attempt to kiss a girl. I was not just waiting for some obvious sign that she wanted it, I was waiting until I could honestly tell myself I was in love with her, and she with me.

Lucky for me, I only ever reached that level with one girl. She must have had a similar guideline for herself, because we were each other's first kiss.

I also decided that an arm around the shoulder meant "I like you," and that holding hands meant "I really like you!"

John Bytheway explained this principle very well:

> Suppose you are on a date, and you put your arm around your date's shoulder. This is a common gesture of affection, but what does it communicate?
>
> How about, "I like you"?
>
> What if you hold hands with your date? That's perhaps a stronger message, isn't it? Maybe that's like saying "I really like you."
>
> Finally, what if you kiss your date? Then what are you saying? What do kisses mean, anyway?
>
> Expressions of affection, like putting your arm around someone's shoulder, holding hands, or giving a kiss good night, involve the principle of honesty. Elder Bruce C. Hafen of the Seventy cautioned young adults to make sure their actions match their intent: "During the time of courtship, please be emotionally honest in the expression of affection. Sometimes you are not as careful as you might be about when, how, and to whom you express your feelings of affection. You must realize that the desire to express affection can be motivated by other things than true love."
>
> If you are emotionally honest you should mean what you say but also mean what you do. Because our expressions of affection send such powerful messages, they involve powerful feelings. Elder Hafen continued: "When any of you—men or women—are given entrance to the heart of a trusting young friend, you stand on holy ground. In such a place you must be honest with yourself—and with your friend—about love and the expression of its symbols. . . .
>
> "Remember, before you are married, you will be more respected and more attractive for the affection you withhold than for the affection you give."[5]

In another talk, Elder Hafen said:

> As Erich Fromm put it, "Desire can be stimulated by the anxiety of aloneness, by the wish to conquer or be conquered, by vanity, by the wish to hurt and even to destroy, as much as it can be stimulated

by love. It seems that sexual desire can easily blend with and be stimulated by any strong emotion, of which love is only one. Because sexual desire is in the minds of most people coupled with the idea of love, they are easily misled to conclude that they love each other when they want each other physically. . . . [But] if [this] desire . . . is not stimulated by love, . . . it . . . leaves strangers as far apart as they were before—sometimes it makes them ashamed of each other, or even makes them hate each other, because when the illusion has gone they feel their estrangement even more markedly than before."

In short, save your kisses—you might need them someday. And when any of you—men or women—are given entrance to the heart of a trusting young friend, you stand on holy ground. In such a place you must be honest with yourself—and with your friend—about love and the expression of its symbols.[6]

I also made some decisions about what I wanted to get out of the first few dates with a girl, and I would recommend these to anyone, since most people commonly accept them.

THE FIRST THREE DATES

A first date is always just a fun date—no commitments and no obligations other than strictly keeping Church standards and having a great time together. The same goes for the second date. Don't stress out on the first two dates. First dates almost always go badly, and sometimes second dates make up for them.

After the second date, consider your feelings. Does this person seem like one you might consider going out with regularly? Of course from the start you should be watching for any red flags that might signal that this person would not be a good marriage candidate, but don't concentrate on marriage. Odds are you won't end up marrying this person anyway, so just have fun.

After the third date, however, you need to decide whether you want to keep dating this person. If you're not sure and feel that maybe there could be some kind of potential, keep dating—that's what dating is for, to discover who you might want to marry. A person ought not to expect much commitment or feedback in the first three dates. But if after three dates, you know you don't want to keep dating this person, then don't go out with them again.

Once you know you don't want to keep dating this person, it is your responsibility to ensure that you don't go on any more dates with them. To do so is to lead them on. To do so is to give them false hopes and expectations. It is your responsibility to break it off, and the longer you wait, the more it will hurt them. The choice is not whether or not to hurt them, the choice is whether to hurt them a little or to wait and hurt them a lot.

BREAKING UP IS *NOT* RUDE

This brings up another important point. You must understand that breaking off a relationship when you know it won't work is not rude. Let me say that again and in simpler language: breaking up with someone is *not* rude! I've heard so many girls say that they can't bring themselves to break up with a guy because they don't want to be rude. IT'S NOT RUDE! In fact, in the long run it's rather kind—painful, but kind. If you do not want the relationship to continue, it is more rude to continue it.

Think about it. Putting off an inevitable breakup is like waiting until the day before prom to call it off. While you're wasting that person's time, he could be seeking other potential dates who might not be available later. Your delay may keep him from finding someone afterward.

Of course, all relationships have ups and downs, and most lasting relationships begin with many questions of continuing the relationship, but when it's clear that things can't ultimately last between you, there is only one answer: the courtship must end. It is not a matter of rudeness and kindness. It's a matter of infinite consequence. We're talking about eternal marriage, not superficial etiquette. If someone asks you on a date, and he isn't a member of the Church, it is not rude to say no. If you know this person could never, under any circumstances, persuade you one day to marry him, it is not the least bit unkind to turn down the first date.

ANY WORTHY PERSON DESERVES A FIRST DATE

Having said that, I also feel that anyone who is a decent person, especially those who are temple worthy, ought to be allowed at least one date if he asks for one. A first date is not a commitment to the person. It's just a date.

Some people never go on dates simply because they are always turned down. Remember, a first date is not a commitment. It never has been, and no one should expect it to be. So use that date as practice if you know you're not interested in this person. Have a great time, and help the other person to have a great time. It may help him have just enough confidence to try it again with someone else. If the date doesn't go too badly, and he's a decent person, you may want to consider allowing him to take you out a second and third time. Who knows, maybe your feelings will change. But I would never go beyond a third date unless you feel that there is some chance this relationship might progress. If there's not a chance, don't go out with him again.

BEAUTY IS IN THE EYE OF GOD

I'm not sure where media came up with the idea that beauty has something to do with weight, but it's not true. Actually, I think media has knowingly taken upon itself the role to make sure that the general population is ugly. In reality, they know nothing about beauty at all. The problem is, they've convinced us that their "standards" of beauty should be sought at all costs.

As a rather plain-looking guy, I've thought a lot about this. The world creates totally meaningless standards that can only be met by the consumption of products and services that only it can provide. The only way they can keep the demand so disgustingly high is to make sure that 90 percent of the population is way below the expectation.

All the while, God keeps telling us, "Look not on his countenance, or on the height of his stature; . . . for the Lord seeth not as man seeth; for man looketh on the outward appearance, but the Lord looketh on the heart" (1 Samuel 16:7).

Of course, the world has to make itself louder than the voice of the Spirit in order to maintain its powerful status. But beauty is *not* in the eye of the beholder. It is in the eye of God. God cares nothing about physical attractiveness, but he does care a great deal about the beauty that comes of bearing children, which naturally causes some flabbiness and increase of skin and weight.

Have you ever noticed that a mother carries a brightness in her eyes that is beautiful and unique to mothers? It first shows up when she is pregnant. Those who know the feature can often figure out she is pregnant before the slightest roundness in the belly begins to show. And it's beautiful! So why do we not see it? For the same reason that we turn our heads at the sound of a coin drop while not noticing the dozens of bird songs surrounding us. The world has done its job well, training us that beauty is in features that it has chosen, and we're the unhappy recipients of its lies. There's a reason that satan is called the father of lies, as well as the prince of this world. He directs the world in its quest to keep the population depressed.

But you can be the exception. You can learn to see beyond the world's ridiculous aspirations and see beauty, including your own, as God sees it! The moment you ask God for His view on things, He'll open to you a whole new vision that is so much more beautiful, so much more exciting, and so much more fulfilling than *anything* the world has to offer.

Once you see things in this way, you may glance back and see several clamoring for another lost pound, another lost wrinkle, or another face-lift. There's a reason those clamorers are depressed. There's a reason they can never seem to grasp what dangles just before them at every moment, and it's not because they are too ugly or too fat, or even too sinful. It is simply because they have let satan distract them from something that he can *never* have—true, eternal beauty.

Under his direction, the world shouts, "You're too baggy, you're hideous, and you're too wrinkly!" All the while he is silently scared to death that you will notice the real beauty that is in you, because the moment you see that, he has no power over you.

That is the moment when life becomes grand and beautiful.

That's the moment you realize that you're already living your "happily ever after." That's the moment you realize that your dreams are already being fulfilled.

Don't let satan distract you from that. God knows who you really are and is anxiously waiting for you to ask Him about it. He wants to explain it to you. You may know it already in theory, and you may have heard it over and over in Sunday School, but you should hear His personal explanation of it to you. I promise it's worth asking.

And don't let up until He tells you everything.

NOTES

1. Lynn G. Robbins, "Agency and Love in Marriage," *Ensign*, Oct. 2000, 16.
2. Lowell L. Bennion "Q&A: Questions and Answers—How Much Kissing Is Too Much?" *New Era*, Feb. 1971, 5.
3. M. Gawain Wells, "Breaking Up without Going to Pieces: When Dating Doesn't End in Marriage," *Ensign*, June 1982, 58.
4. Spencer W. Kimball, *The Teachings of Spencer W. Kimball*, ed. Edward L. Kimball (Salt Lake City: Bookcraft, 1995), 281.
5. John Bytheway, "What Do Kisses Mean?" *New Era*, Oct. 2004, 39.
6. Hafen, "The Gospel and Romantic Love."

fifteen

~

Dinner Date

I was working in a quiet little section in the back corner of Deseret Book. Then I remembered that this coming Friday was the annual Deseret Book banquet. It usually took place at some fancy restaurant with the company paying for it. A sign-up sheet was in the office to let the company know whether you would be coming and if you were bringing a guest. We were invited to bring one guest, and I had planned on bringing my brother, though I hadn't mentioned it to him yet. I also hadn't signed the list yet, so seeing that my corner of the store was clear of customers, I left my post and walked into the office.

When I stepped inside, two frenzied employees, both girls about my age, immediately accosted me. "Chas, are you taking a date to the dinner Friday night?"

Taken aback, and wondering if they were wasting their guest offer by inviting *me*, I fumbled, "Uh . . . well . . . I . . ."

"Because we both want to bring one, but we don't want to be the only ones with dates! Tamra's bringing her sister, Marcy is bringing one of her girl friends, and Michael is bringing his brother. We don't want to bring dates if we're the only ones! Are you bringing a date?"

"Well, uh . . . I suppose I could. But that's tomorrow evening, I'm not sure if I can get someone that soon. I could try."

"Good!" they replied, "we don't have dates yet either, but we didn't want to get them until we knew for sure that someone else was planning on it."

"Okay," I said. "I guess I'll bring a date too, then."

"Awesome!"

I signed my name on the list and wrote, "Date" next to it.

After leaving the office, I felt like banging my head into a wall. I didn't have a girlfriend, and I wasn't about to dial the number of every girl I knew just to get a short-notice date. Why had I promised to try? Why couldn't I just say, "I'll think about it," or "If you want to set me up with someone," or something? At least that way I wouldn't have to go through the trauma of asking someone out, especially to an event where most people would not have dates.

By the time I arrived at school the next morning, I felt a little nauseous. I didn't want to go through with the deal. I had never asked someone out the day of the date. Maybe I could just ask someone who I knew was working that night so I would be able to say I had tried. I had arrived at class a little early in hopes of bumping into someone I knew so I could conveniently ask them out. But I couldn't picture myself doing that. That wasn't my style, and it was certainly *way* out of my comfort zone. What had I gotten myself into?

As I walked into my music theory class, one of the girls in the class shouted, "Chas!"

I looked up. All the girls in the class (most of the members of that class were girls) looked at me while the one who had shouted my name continued, "You're a guy! You want to go on a date?"

"What?"

"I was just telling everyone that my boyfriend gets home from his mission in a week! I made a goal when he left to go on a hundred dates while he was gone. I'm only five short!"

I was shocked and nearly laughed out loud. "Sure! How about dinner tonight? I need a date for a banquet, and I didn't know who to ask."

"Are you serious?"

"Sure, if you are."

"Cool!" she said, clapping her hands. "I just might make my goal!"

We had a great time. In fact, it was one of the less stressful dates I had been on because it was just for the sake of a goal.

sixteen

The "C" Word

Boyd K. Packer said:

Young people sometimes get the mistaken notion that spirituality and the religious attitude interfere with youthful growth. They assume that the requirements of the Church are interferences and aggravations which thwart the full expression of young manhood and young womanhood.

How foolish is the youth who feels that the Church is a fence around love to keep him out. Oh, youth, if you could know! The requirements of the Church are the highway to love and to happiness, with guardrails securely in place, with guideposts plainly marked, and with help along the way. How unfortunate to resent counsel and restraint! How fortunate are you who follow the standards of the Church, even if just from sheer obedience or habit! You will find a rapture and a joy fulfilled.[1]

THE DEVIL'S PLAN

In the gospel, we talk a lot about the plan of salvation, otherwise known as God's plan. But have you ever wondered what satan's plan is? What does he consider his own purpose to be? He has an agenda. Want to know what it is?

Elder Packer said, "The single purpose of Lucifer is to oppose the great plan of happiness, to corrupt the purest, most beautiful, and appealing experiences of life: romance, love, marriage, and parenthood."[2]

Hang on! Hit the breaks! You're saying that the devil's whole plan is to ruin families? That's what it sounds like to me. Why would he care? Well, for one thing, he'll never get one. You know what else he'll never get? A body. And he seems pretty bent to destroy our bodies and families.

So . . . from the devil's perspective: you want to destroy the families and bodies of God's children—what do you do? Obviously you have no power to physically damage their bodies, since you don't have one yourself. You'll have to get them to destroy their *own* bodies. How do you do that?

The devil is a tricky fellow. If you think about it, most sins come from misuse of something that is innately good. A perfect example of this is the sin of immorality. The Lord gives us the law of chastity, not because sex is bad, but because it is so good. Sex is wonderful and beautiful. In fact, it's one of the few celestial capacities God has given us in this life. Properly used, this gift strengthens marriages and creates life.

But because of this, the misuse of this divine gift is deadly, spiritually speaking, and in some instances, physically deadly as well.

Elder Bruce C. Hafen said:

> Properly understood, then, the scriptures counsel us to be virtuous not because romantic love is bad, but precisely because romantic love is so good. It is not only good; it is pure, precious, even sacred and holy. For that reason, one of Satan's cheapest and dirtiest tricks is to make profane that which is sacred. Building on a metaphor from President Harold B. Lee, it is as though Satan holds up to the world a degraded image of sexual love suggested by imagining the drunken, boisterous laughter of filthy men in a brothel, located on some crowded, dusty highway of life, where the flower of fair womanhood is jeered at, dirtied, brutalized, and ultimately crushed with unclean hands. Meanwhile, far, far away from the madding crowd, high up in the cool protected valleys of tall mountains, grows the priceless flower of virtue—untarnished, pure, and unsullied. It waits as a noble prize for those valiant few who are willing to climb to its heights by paying the price of patience, obedience, and a lifetime of devotion—an endless, unselfish loyalty to spouse and children.[3]

Have you ever wondered why the scriptures place immorality next to murder in seriousness? Elder Holland explained,

> Setting aside sins against the Holy Ghost for a moment as a special category unto themselves, it is LDS doctrine that sexual transgression is second only to murder in the Lord's list of life's most serious sins. By assigning such rank to illicit indulgence in a physical appetite so conspicuously evident in all of us, what is God trying to tell us about its place in His plan for all men and women in mortality? I submit to you He is doing precisely that—commenting about the very plan of life itself. Clearly God's greatest concerns regarding mortality are how one gets into this world and how one gets out of it. These two most important issues in our very personal and carefully supervised progress are the two issues that He as our Creator and Father and Guide wishes most to reserve to himself. These are the two matters that He has repeatedly told us He wants us never to take illegally, illicitly, unfaithfully, without sanction.[4]

Elder Hafen said almost the same thing.

> Sometimes we give as reasons for the law of chastity the risk of pregnancy or abortion, the possibility of an unwanted or embarrassing marriage, or the chance of a terrible venereal disease. With adultery, we talk about the damage of destroying an existing marriage or family. As serious as these things are, I'm not sure they are the fundamental reason for the Lord's having placed this commandment ahead of armed robbery and fraud in the seriousness of sins.
>
> Think of it—unchastity is second only to murder. Perhaps there is a common element in those two things—unchastity and murder. Both have to do with life, which touches upon the highest of divine powers. Murder involves the wrongful taking of life; sexual transgression may involve the wrongful giving of life, or the wrongful tampering with the sacred fountains of life-giving power.[5]

THE GIFT OF REPENTANCE

Of course, when we speak of morality, it is important to talk about repentance. All of us need repentance, and it is rarely, if ever, easy. It hurts. But, oh, how liberating it is! The joy and fulfillment that comes from true repentance is worth any embarrassment that may come in the process. Some sins only require forsaking the sin and sincerely praying for forgiveness while others require confession. And how do you know if your sins require confession?

One good rule of thumb is if it is a sin of a moral nature (chastity), whether tampering with someone else's body or with your own body, it ought to be confessed to your bishop. Any intentional contact with the sacred parts of another's body, with or without clothing, ought to be confessed. If you have any question about whether or not your sins require confession, just do it.

Your bishop can tell you what you need to do next. He is much more loving and compassionate than you may think. He's a servant of God. It's a heavy mantle to act as a judge in Israel, to carry the burden of discerning the seriousness of your sins, and he knows it. He will not treat that role lightly. He will do all he needs to in order to obtain inspiration for counseling and helping you to overcome your sin. He wants more than anything to see you make the changes that will turn you into a better, happier, more Christlike person.

Most of all, your bishop *knows* the Lord. Perhaps you are expecting that he will react with shock or disappointment. He won't. The Lord has prepared him for his role, and likely the Spirit has already told him a great deal. Don't be afraid tell him your feelings and follow his counsel. Confession is for you, and whether or not it's your "way" of dealing with things, it is the Lord's way, and no matter what excuse you may have for Him, His ways are higher than yours. His ways are always better for you than your own ways. I guarantee that.

Perhaps you feel nervous *thinking* about confessing. Maybe it makes you feel uneasy or uncomfortable to even think about telling the bishop about your problems. If so, don't think about it. Just do it. Just call him up or make an appointment to see him, and then don't think about it. Just tell him everything. You'll find that it's easier and more comfortable than you anticipated, and the burden will lift from your spirit, filling you with hope and courage.

You should keep one thing in mind if you have been involved in sin and are making your way back: it may take some time for you to become and feel clean and whole again. That's okay. It's normal. Just recognize that this "probation" time may put serious dating on hold. If your girlfriend or boyfriend was involved in your transgression, but there was no pregnancy, then you probably should break up. You have already proven to each other that neither of you can be trusted at the present time. Just break it off to give yourself time to change and rebuild your self-respect and self-discipline.

This may also mean it's probably not the best time to be seeking out a new dating partner. If she is a good, faithful member of the Church, she is probably looking for someone who is temple worthy. That is *not* judgmental of her—it is good, wise, and right. Never get upset with the faithful for seeking someone who is already prepared to go to the temple, just do all that is necessary to become such a person. Sometimes *time* is part of the repentance process. Don't lower your own standards of wanting to marry in the temple simply because you may not be worthy at present. Just get that way before actively pursuing marriage.

Recognize that some consequences of your transgressions will continue to be a trial throughout your life, even after you've repented and become temple worthy again. It would be ridiculous to expect all consequences to be eliminated with forgiveness. The Savior's Atonement will heal and cleanse you completely. It will assist you in every aspect of your life—including receiving the strength to endure the natural consequences of your past (albeit forgiven) transgressions. Stay close to the Lord, face up to the consequences with courage, and determine to stay on the Lord's side of the line from now on. Don't knock the faithful for never having experienced the depth of the repentance process that you have experienced. They may not have the context you have, but they have the same determination to keep the commandments and endure to the end.

I am deeply impressed by many who have made amazing comebacks after committing or living in sin. They have tasted the bitterness, and now they savor the sweet. It was never intended that we carry the burden of our sins through life. God wants us to be cleansed of them now. Not only will you find that the Lord is willing to forgive even you, but you will also find strength and testimony expanding, and your fears will vanish as if they were never there. The Lord knows of your fears, and he wants to take them away, but you have to make that first step.

Sin Doesn't Make You Stronger

Having said all that, it's important to understand that it is better to remain faithful than to fall away and come back. Some think that it is better to be involved in sin and then come out victorious, as if they will be stronger than they would if they had never fallen into sin. This is a false assumption.

Spencer W. Kimball once said:

> Another error into which some transgressors fall, because of the availability of God's forgiveness, is the illusion that they are somehow stronger for having committed sin and then lived through the period of repentance. This simply is not true. That man who resists temptation and lives without sin is far better off than the man who has fallen, no matter how repentant the latter may be. The reformed transgressor, it is true, may be more understanding of one who falls into the same sin, and to that extent perhaps more helpful in the latter's regeneration. But his sin and repentance have certainly not made him stronger than the consistently righteous person.[6]

Why would that be? Why would someone who is consistently faithful—who hasn't had to trudge through sin or overcome almost impossible odds—be stronger than those who have lived through the whole cleansing process?

C.S. Lewis said:

> A silly idea is current that good people do not know what temptation means. This is an obvious lie. Only those who try to resist temptation know how strong it is. . . . A man who gives in to temptation after five minutes simply does not know what it would have been like an hour later. That is why bad people, in one sense, know very little about badness. They have lived a sheltered life by always giving in. We never find out the strength of the evil impulse inside us until we try to fight it.[7]

I sometimes want to laugh when people say that we, as members of God's church, live a sheltered life. If the life of a faithful Latter-day Saint can be called sheltered, then it's the shelter that comes from fighting off every enemy. If an undefeated boxer can be called sheltered simply because he can't be beaten down, then what do we call those who are beaten? Open-minded? I once heard someone say that there is a big difference between an open mind and a hole in the head. Someone else once told me, "Don't have your mind so open that your brain falls out."

IMMORALITY IS BAD BECAUSE INTIMACY IS GOOD

It's important to recognize that temptation can be terribly strong, especially with something as good, powerful, and holy as physical intimacy. Sex is not an evil thing. It is a remarkably good and sacred thing of beauty. And because intimacy is so sacred, using it unlawfully is terribly bad. If we think it is not a thing of great consequence, it is because we don't know how sacred it is.

One reason sex can be so dangerous before marriage is that after a person has been sexually active, the body craves it much stronger than before. In marriage, this desire is good, and it strengthens the relationship because a couple can freely share that experience together often. Outside of marriage, it can drive a person to act in ways they would have previously thought unthinkable.

Will and Ariel Durant, who were Pulitzer prize-winning authors and philosophers, said:

> No one man [or woman], however brilliant or well-informed, can come in one lifetime to such fullness of understanding as to safely judge and dismiss the customs or institutions of his society, for these are the wisdom of generations after centuries of experiment in the laboratory of history. A youth boiling with hormones will wonder why he should not give full freedom to his sexual desires; and if he is unchecked by custom, morals, or laws, he may ruin his life [or hers] before he matures sufficiently to understand that sex is a river of fire that must be banked and cooled by a hundred restraints if it is not to consume in chaos both the individual and the group.[8]

How do you control your hormones? You don't toy with them. You don't see how far you can safely go without losing control. You make conscious decisions and then stick to those decisions. Make the resolution, "I will not participate in sexual behavior of any kind outside of marriage. And when I am married, it will be *only* with my spouse." Is that an unrealistic goal? Is it impractical? God said it's not. If you want to argue with God, take it up with Him—but know that no matter how you argue, He's still right. It is neither impractical nor unrealistic to live the law of chastity completely. But it is impractical and even impossible to break the law of chastity without hurting yourself and your partner—no exceptions.

Bruce C. Hafen said:

> Develop the power of self-discipline and self-restraint. Please remember that nobody ever fell off a cliff who never went near one. You've got to be like Joseph, not like David. When Potiphar's wife tried to seduce him, the scripture says, Joseph "fled, and got him out" (Genesis 39:12). Joseph knew that it is wiser to avoid temptation than to resist it. King David, by contrast, somehow developed too much confidence in his own ability to handle temptation. He was tragically willing to flirt—to flirt with evil, and it ultimately destroyed him. In your courtships, even when you feel there is a growing foundation of true love, show your profound respect for that love and the possibilities of your life together by restraining your passions. Please don't be deceived by the false notion that anything short of the sex act itself is acceptable conduct. That is a lie, not only because one step overpoweringly leads to another, but also because the handling of another's body is in an important sense part of the sexual act that is kept holy by the sanctuary of chastity. If ever you are in doubt about where the line is between love and lust, draw the line toward the side of love. Nobody ever fell off a cliff who never went near one.[9]

I'd like to share one more quote about physical intimacy, and I'll warn you: it's a long one, but it's worth reading every word—perhaps multiple times, if it helps. This is Jeffrey R. Holland, from his talk called "Of Souls, Symbols, and Sacraments":

> As delicate as it is to mention in such a setting, I nevertheless trust your maturity to understand that physiologically we are created

as men and women to fit together in such a union. In this ultimate physical expression of one man and one woman they are as nearly and as literally "one" as two separate physical bodies can ever be. It is in that act of ultimate physical intimacy we most nearly fulfill the commandment of the Lord given to Adam and Eve, living symbols for all married couples, when He invited them to cleave unto one another only, and thus become "one flesh" (Genesis 2:24).

Obviously, such a commandment to these two, the first husband and wife of the human family, has unlimited implications—social, cultural, and religious as well as physical—but that is exactly my point. As all couples come to that moment of bonding in mortality, it is intended to be just such a complete union. That commandment cannot be fulfilled, and that symbolism of "one flesh" cannot be preserved, if we hastily and guiltily and surreptitiously share intimacy in a darkened corner of a darkened hour, then just as hastily and guiltily and surreptitiously retreat to our separate worlds—not to eat or live or cry or laugh together, not to do the laundry and the dishes and the homework, not to manage a budget and pay the bills and tend the children and plan together for the future. No, we cannot do that until we are truly one-united, bound, linked, tied, welded, sealed, married.

Can you see then the moral schizophrenia that comes from pretending we are one, sharing the physical symbols and physical intimacy of our union, but then fleeing, retreating, severing all such other aspects—and symbols—of what was meant to be a total obligation, only to unite again furtively some other night or, worse yet, furtively unite (and you can tell how cynically I use that word) with some other partner who is no more bound to us, no more one with us than the last was or than the one that will come next week or next month or next year or anytime before the binding commitments of marriage?

You must wait—you must wait until you can give everything, and you cannot give everything until you are at least legally and, for Latter-day Saint purposes, eternally pronounced as one. To give illicitly that which is not yours to give (remember—"you are not your own") and to give only part of that which cannot be followed with the gift of your whole heart and your whole life and your whole self is its own form of emotional Russian roulette. If you persist in sharing part without the whole, in pursuing satisfaction devoid of symbolism, in giving parts and pieces and inflamed fragments only, you run the terrible risk of such spiritual, psychic damage that you may undermine both your physical intimacy and your wholehearted devotion to a truer, later love. You may come to that moment of real love, of total union, only to discover to your horror that what you should have saved has been spent, and mark my words—only God's grace can recover that piecemeal dissipation of your virtue.[10]

One of the reasons we have to be so careful in dating is that our thoughts determine a great deal about the state of our worthiness. We have to watch our thoughts very carefully and never do anything that arouses the sexual feelings and thoughts inside.

There is a reason for that. As President Spencer W. Kimball taught:

> Thoughts largely determine immorality of acts. Holding hands would generally not be immoral, but it would depend on whether or not one's mind ran rampant. An embrace may not be immoral, but if the closeness of the body awakens immoral desires, then that is another thing. "As [a man] thinketh . . . so is he." (Proverbs 23:7.) "Unto the pure all things are pure: but unto them that are defiled and unbelieving is nothing pure." (Titus 1:15.) One must keep the thoughts clean. . . . Two people could embrace, kiss, dance, look, and I can conceive of one of them being immoral and the other innocent of sin.[11]

PORNOGRAPHY

One of the most common violations of the law of chastity is the viewing of pornography. Pornography is a serious form of immorality and can be just as damaging and addicting as alcohol or heroin. Dallin H. Oaks, speaking of pornography, said, "It impairs decision-making capacities and it 'hooks' its users, drawing them back obsessively for more and more. A man who had been addicted to pornography and to hard drugs wrote me this comparison: 'In my eyes cocaine doesn't hold a candle to this. I have done both. . . . Quitting even the hardest drugs was nothing compared to [trying to quit pornography]" (letter of Mar. 20, 2005).[12]

Pornography is an abuse of the sacred inclinations that are

intended to bring good people together into a family unit. Don't give in to any degree of temptation in this matter—it will win. Of course you have self-discipline, but the moment you give in to the temptation to momentarily glance, you have forfeited that self-discipline just long enough for the temptation to take root, and that moment can become a permanent scar on the spirit. That scar can become infected and spread like a virus into all aspects of your life, corrupting all that was once good.

Dallin H. Oaks said:

> Pornographic or erotic stories and pictures are worse than filthy or polluted food. The body has defenses to rid itself of unwholesome food. With a few fatal exceptions, bad food will only make you sick but do no permanent harm. In contrast, a person who feasts upon filthy stories or pornographic or erotic pictures and literature records them in this marvelous retrieval system we call a brain. The brain won't vomit back filth. Once recorded, it will always remain subject to recall, flashing its perverted images across your mind and drawing you away from the wholesome things in life.[13]

How does an otherwise good, faithful person become enslaved by such a vile, corrosive disease? We know from the scriptures that "the natural man is an enemy to God, and has been from the fall of Adam, and will be, forever and ever, unless he yields to the enticings of the Holy Spirit, and putteth off the natural man and becometh a saint through the atonement of Christ the Lord, and becometh as a child, submissive, meek, humble, patient, full of love" (Mosiah 3:19).

If your body has a natural inclination to do something that is wrong, then you must *not* give in to that inclination. The key is to recognize these "natural man" tendencies before they lead you to making a wrong choice. If a picture pops up on the Internet that you should not look at, immediately make the choice not to look, and get off that page. If you're walking down the street and see someone dressed immodestly, look away. When you do, the Lord will strengthen you to fight off evil thoughts. If you choose to look, however, you will lose the Spirit, and once the Spirit is gone, you'll find that your power to resist evil thoughts will be considerably weakened.

There's an old poem by John Bartlett that goes:

> *Vice is a monster of so frightful mien*
> *As to be hated needs but to be seen;*
> *Yet seen too oft, familiar with her face,*
> *We first endure, then pity, then embrace.*[14]

All it takes to become enslaved by temptation is to give in to small, seemingly insignificant temptations. Do you want to be trapped by your own weakness?

Dallin H. Oaks counseled:

> Don't accommodate any degree of temptation. Prevent sin and avoid having to deal with its inevitable destruction. So, turn it off! Look away! Avoid it at all costs. Direct your thoughts in wholesome paths. Remember your covenants and be faithful in temple attendance. The wise bishop I quoted earlier reported that "an endowed priesthood bearer's fall into pornography never occurs during periods of regular worship in the temple; it happens when he has become casual in his temple worship" (letter of Mar. 13, 2005)."[15]

If you have already given in to this temptation or weakened yourself by allowing little "natural man" tendencies to control you, recognize the fact. Recognize the problem. Do *not* make excuses. That is like welding closed an escape hatch. Remember that guilt is a good and healthy thing if it leads you to change for the better. Don't excuse your wrongful actions or thoughts.

Dallin H. Oaks continued:

> Some seek to justify their indulgence by arguing that they are only viewing "soft," not "hard," porn. A wise bishop called this refusing to see evil as evil. He quoted men seeking to justify their viewing choices by comparisons such as "not as bad as" or "only one bad scene." But the test of what is evil is not its degree but its effect. When persons entertain evil thoughts long enough for the Spirit to withdraw, they lose their spiritual protection and they are subject to the power and direction of the evil one. When they use Internet or other pornography for what this bishop described as "arousal on demand" (letter of Mar. 13, 2005), they are deeply soiled by sin.[16]

If you are already involved in pornography, determine to change right now—don't wait another moment. Change *now*, then pray for the strength and courage to overcome the problem. Then go to your bishop. Don't *think* about going to your bishop—just go to him. He can and will help.

IMMODESTY

We have spoken of immorality and pornography, but we ought to be aware of one other branch of chastity. Thomas S. Monson, speaking on this topic, said, "When I consider the demons who are twins—even immodesty and immorality—I should make them triplets and include pornography. They all three go together."[17]

While pornography is more often a problem among boys, immodesty is more often a problem among girls. Why is immodesty such an issue? Shouldn't a girl be able to wear what she wants?

It's important to realize that there is a correlation between pornography and immodesty. Elder Oaks, in the same talk quoted above, said, "Young women, please understand that if you dress immodestly, you are magnifying this problem by becoming pornography to some of the men who see you."[18]

A young man has no excuse whatsoever for involvement in pornography, or even for improper thoughts or feelings toward a girl. He must take the full initiative for his own spiritual safety, and if he does not, he *will* be overcome. He must understand that. He can never blame a girl for his improper thoughts or intentions, no matter what she says, wears, or does. He is responsible for his own spiritual standing. No one can be blamed for any sin he commits.

Having said that, I think it's important for girls to understand what they are putting guys through when they dress immodestly. How would it make you feel if you learned that a righteous, faithful young man was desperately fighting inside to keep his thoughts clean, simply because of your choice of outfit? To a girl, an immodest outfit may be cute and stylish, but to a faithful young man, it may be a massive spiritual danger. If he is a good, faithful young man who wants to keep the Spirit, he will probably get out of your presence as soon as possible. You have become to him an unholy place, because his thoughts can't be clean around you without a strong inner battle. He would be unwise to stay. If you're on a date with him, you are placing an unfair burden on him.

His intentions of leaving your presence do not mean he is being judgmental. His leaving your presence is his desperate attempt to maintain a clean mind. Though he may lose some respect or trust in you, he won't consider you an evil person for what you wear. But know that he will probably not seek your interest in the future.

The irony is that while your immodest dress will scare off a faithful young man, it will quickly attract an *un*faithful young man. He doesn't watch his thoughts, and your clothing will lure him in. Is that the kind of person you want pursuing you?

Many women recognize the incredible physical influence they have on men and use it to their advantage. Know that you will be held accountable for any suffering and temptation you intentionally cause a righteous young man.

Many women do not recognize what a challenge this is for young men. Well, now you know.

To a pure, faithful young man, modesty is more attractive than you may think. A righteous young man knows his feelings and the incredible power of physical attraction, and he wants a girl with whom he can feel spiritually safe. He knows that all of his inclinations will be fulfilled in marriage, and he is willing and determined to wait. When he finds a girl who recognizes her own power and handles it modestly and righteously, he feels spiritually comfortable with her and will be more ready to ask the girl out and make the commitments that lead to marriage. And if you can find a young man like that, you will find the pureness and faithfulness that he strives so hard to maintain will serve you again and again and again.

NOTES

1. Boyd K. Packer, "You're in the Driver's Seat," *New Era,* June 2004, 5.
2. Boyd K. Packer, "For Time and All Eternity," *Ensign,* Nov. 1993.
3. Hafen, "The Gospel and Romantic Love," 10.
4. Jeffrey R. Holland, "Of Souls, Symbols, and Sacraments," in *Brigham Young University 1987–88 Devotional and Fireside Speeches* (1988), 78–79.
5. Hafen, "The Gospel and Romantic Love," 10.
6. Spencer W. Kimball, *The Miracle of Forgiveness* (Salt Lake City: Bookcraft, 1969), 357.
7. C. S. Lewis, *The Complete C. S. Lewis Signature Classics* (New York, HarperCollins, 2002), 78.
8. Will and Ariel Durant, *The Lessons of History* (New York: Simon and Schuster, 1968), 35–36.
9. Hafen, "The Gospel and Romantic Love," 10.
10. Holland, "Of Souls, Symbols, and Sacraments," 78–79.
11. *The Teachings of Spencer W. Kimball,* 282.
12. Dallin H. Oaks, "Pornography," *Ensign,* May 2005, 87–90.
13. Ibid.
14. John Bartlett, *Familiar Quotations* (Boston: Little Brown and Co., 1968), 409.
15. Oaks, "Pornography," 87–90.
16. Ibid.
17. Thomas S. Monson, "Peace, Be Still," *Ensign,* Nov. 2002, 53–56.
18. Oaks, "Pornography," 87–90.

seventeen

Top 5 List

Talking about marriage, Patricia Holland said: "When young people have visited with Sister Camilla Kimball about how wonderful it must be to be married to a prophet, she has said, 'Yes, it is wonderful, but I didn't marry a prophet. I just married a returned missionary.'"[1]

I had a top five list—the important things that a girl needed if I were to even consider marrying her. They were my non-negotiables. It took me about a year to develop this list, but I wanted to get it right. I knew that deciding who to marry would be the most important decision of my life. I couldn't make a mistake in that choice, no matter how imperfect I was.

In coming up with my top five list, I made sure to put it all in the order of importance, number one being the most important.

5. She is the type of girl that would support me in whatever church callings I might have.

4. She loves and respects family—both mine and hers.

3. She loves children, wants to be a mother, and hopes, if possible, to be a full-time mother.

2. She loves the temple and is worthy to hold a temple recommend.

1. She loves the Lord more than she loves me.

5. She Is the Type of Girl that Would Support Me in Whatever Church Callings I Might Have

I doubted I would ever have any huge calling in the church, but to me, faithfulness in my callings had a bearing on my personal relationship with the Savior. I needed to find someone who could support and encourage me in that relationship.

4. She Loves and Respects Family—Both Mine and Hers

Most of us have heard it said that if you want to know how a man will treat his wife, observe how he treats his mother. The same is true of how a woman treats her father. In addition, the way she treats younger siblings, nieces, and nephews can tell a lot about how a girl will treat her own children. If she cares for them and treats them with respect and love, she's likely to be such a mother. If she shouts at them or treats them like dirt, she'll probably do the same with her own children. Besides, the members of my family had always been my best friends, and if she couldn't at least respect those who I was close to, how could she really get close to me?

3. She Loves Children, Wants to be a Mother, and Hopes, If Possible, to be a Full-time Mother

I have always loved children. There were few hopes that thrilled me more than the thought of having my own children. What a great honor that would be. What a responsibility. What a joy! I knew I was not only looking for a wife, but I was also looking for a mother for my children, someone I could trust with my posterity, someone I trusted enough to be assured that my children would be in good hands—the best hands. I took President Hinckley's words seriously when he said to holders of the priesthood:

> Choose carefully and wisely. The girl you marry will be yours forever. You will love her and she will love you through thick and thin, through sunshine and storm. She will become the mother of your children. What greater thing in all this world can there be than to become the father of a precious child, a son or daughter of God,

our Father in Heaven, for whom we are given the rights and responsibilities of mortal stewardship.

How precious a thing is a baby. How wonderful a thing is a
child. What a marvelous thing is a family. Live worthy of becoming
a father of whom your wife and children will be proud.

The Lord has ordained that we should marry, that we shall live
together in love and peace and harmony, that we shall have children
and rear them in His holy ways.[2]

I wanted to find someone who saw it as her greatest purpose in
life to raise, nurture, and teach our children. I knew trying to find a
girl who wanted to be a stay at home mother would be a challenge. It
would be unfair and overbearing on my part to try to *convince* a girl
to be a stay-at-home mother. It wouldn't be my place to attempt that.
I knew that if I wanted a wife who would be a full-time mother, I
would have to find someone who fully desired that for herself.

2. She Loves the Temple and Is Worthy to Hold a Temple Recommend

There is something great to be said for a girl who dedicates herself
to temple worship. Not only is it a great sign of devotion, but it
signifies she's on the path to attain a celestial marriage and family.
Someone who is not worthy of a temple recommend is not on that
path, and unless she is diligently striving to *become* worthy, she's
going some other direction and will never get there without a great
change of heart.

Just as with full-time motherhood, I knew I could not expect to
change a potential spouse to *become* temple worthy at my request.
When it came to finding a wife, I had to find someone who was
already well on that path. If I thought I could encourage her to
change and become temple worthy, I would be making unwise
and blind judgments that may lead to a painful realization that my
family can only be temporary. I knew that if I wanted my family
to last forever, I must choose a woman who is already worthy of a
temple recommend, both for my own sake, and for the sake of my
future children, who may otherwise lose their parents for eternity.

1. SHE LOVES THE LORD MORE THAN SHE LOVES ME

Last and most important of all, she needed to put the Lord first in her life.

Whatever is most important in our lives comes first. It will dictate our every decision. That is why it is so essential we put the Lord first. If He is first, He will see to it that we have the rest of our priorities in order. He will make sure we remember to spend proper time with family, fulfill our roles and callings, give honest time and effort in our jobs, and become what He wants us to become. He will direct us in everything we do. Even if we are not entirely clear about how to get such direction from the Lord, if we put Him first, He will guide us through that process.

I knew if I found a girl who put Him first, we could have a great marriage.

I knew that I needed to consider other important factors finding the right girl to marry. I knew that even someone who has all these attributes might still have other problems that could make our marriage difficult. I tried to consider everything I knew about a girl as I dated her to see if she could be right for me. Sometimes even the small things could lead to big problems. I knew I had to make a decision whenever I discovered new problems.

Such big decisions were almost always the great challenge of my young adult life. They counted for so much, and no matter what choice I made, there were small as well as eternal consequences.

I knew that trying to change a girl in order to marry her was a bad idea. I even tried to think to myself, "If this girl turned out to be a little worse than I think she is, would she still be worth marrying?" I know that sounds pessimistic, but the reality is that after marriage, spouses discover things about each other that they didn't know and don't like. That's inevitable.

I did hope that the flaws I would discover in my wife after we were married would be trivial things. So whenever I began dating someone, I tried to watch for her weaknesses and assumed that the problems were much worse than she was allowing me to see.

I don't think I was being a perfectionist. I knew that I would be marrying a human being, and every human being has a package of problems. I just had to pick which package of problems to marry.

Every person you date will come as a package deal, with gifts, attributes, abilities, weaknesses, and problems. Everyone has them, and when you marry, you marry a person with weaknesses and problems. Expect and accept that, and choose your package wisely. Also, while you're searching, be aware of the flaws and weaknesses in your package. Don't try to hide them, but deal with them appropriately and communicate well with those you date so you can understand and help each other.

I also tried to remember that I was seeking out a daughter of God—an imperfect daughter, but still a daughter of God. I knew that no matter what kinds of problems a girl had, she was a daughter of our Heavenly Father.

BECOMING DATE-WORTHY

John Bytheway said:

> One of the hard lessons to learn in life is that there are some things you can control and some things you can't. If you want a short recipe for being frustrated and miserable, this is it: focus on things you can't control. While you may not be able to "make" someone like you, it is possible to make yourself more "likable." The way to do that is to focus on what you can control. Here are three things you can do, even when you feel like there isn't a friend in sight. You can be curious, you can be clean, and you can be Christlike.[3]

Those three things—be curious, be clean, and be Christlike—are three things you can control, and they really will help you become more dateable.

After developing my top five list, it occurred to me that I had better make sure *I* fit those qualities—otherwise it didn't make a difference whether I met such a girl, because she wouldn't be interested in me. I decided to spend even more effort developing these qualities in myself as I spent searching for a girl who had them. So I adapted the list to help me become the perfect counterpart for the perfect girl.

5. I should be the type of person to support her in

whatever church callings she will receive. I should also support her through whatever callings *I* might receive, and I should accept and fulfill honorably any calling the Lord extended to me.

4. I should love and respect my family and hers.

3. I should love children and want to be a father. I should get myself into a situation where I could fully support a family on one income and still be an active father in our home.

2. I should love the temple, attend often, and always remain worthy to hold a temple recommend.

1. I should love the Lord more than I love her.

My personal top five list not only helped me to focus on *becoming* a good potential husband, but it also helped me learn to focus on what I *can* control. I can't control what a particular girl is like or how she feels about me, but I can certainly control what kind of person *I* am.

My top five list of qualities to look for in a girl helped me look beyond the beautiful faces and charismatic personalities that can easily cloud the most important aspects of a girl's character. I wasn't looking for a girlfriend. I was looking for an eternal companion. I could not and would not make a mistake on that. *After* meeting a girl that met these qualities, I would consider other desirable features, knowing that as long as she met the top five qualities, she would most likely be a fantastic partner.

I knew if I lived up to the qualities I desired in a companion, it would be much easier to find her.

Most of all, it helped me remember to always put the Lord first in my life.

While trying to develop skills that will help you be a great partner, it helps to look beyond the obvious, easily identifiable abilities. You may not be able to compete with the football star in athletic prowess or with Betty Crocker for the best baking abilities, but you can always improve yourself. And while trying to practice your skills at dancing or making people laugh, don't forget that the most attractive features are not always the most apparent.

Jeffrey R. Holland talked about some of the qualities to look for in a date when he said:

> There are lots of limitations in all of us that we hope our sweethearts will overlook. I suppose no one is as handsome or as beautiful as he or she wishes, or as brilliant in school or as witty in speech or as wealthy as we would like, but in a world of varied talents and fortunes that we can't always command, I think that makes even more attractive the qualities we can command—such qualities as thoughtfulness, patience, a kind word, and true delight in the accomplishment of another. These cost us nothing, and they can mean everything to the one who receives them.[4]

GOOD HABITS ARE BETTER THAN GREAT INCOME

One of the more common worries that many young couples have is financial security—a valid concern, since finances can be one of the leading factors in marital contention. But often these concerns are misdirected. While searching for a companion, you may be looking for someone who has a good income or a full bank account, but what you should really be looking for is someone with sound financial tendencies. The poor person who is wise with money has a great deal more to offer in a marriage than a rich person with bad financial habits.

This does not mean a good prospect must know *all* the ins and outs of good financial practices, but it does mean that if a person is thousands of dollars deep in pointless consumer debt, it may be wise to reconsider the relationship. It may seem harsh at the time of separation, but it will save you a lifetime of terrible financial and marital strain or divorce.

Don't be afraid of going into a marriage poor. There's no shame in starting a life together without all the things society expects a married couple to have. Your struggle will get you closer if you stay close to the Lord and put faith in His promises. President Thomas S.

Monson said it this way:

> I realize there are many reasons why you may be hesitating
> to take that step of getting married. If you are concerned about
> providing financially for a wife and family, may I assure you
> that there is no shame in a couple having to scrimp and save. It
> is generally during these challenging times that you will grow
> closer together as you learn to sacrifice and to make difficult
> decisions. Perhaps you are afraid of making the wrong choice.
> To this I say that you need to exercise faith. Find someone with
> whom you can be compatible. Realize that you will not be able
> to anticipate every challenge which may arise, but be assured
> that almost anything can be worked out if you are resourceful
> and if you are committed to making your marriage work.[5]

The same may be said of things like schooling and career
advancement. The point is not to find someone who has finished his
schooling or found employment to carry him through the coming
years, but to find someone who values education and works hard.
Those attributes do far more than a position or a degree.

Don't Be Afraid to Grow Together

Consider another factor in preparation for marriage that is often
overlooked. Some feel that they should wait until they are well established or old enough to think like a well-trained adult before they
seek an eternal companion. The problem with this approach is that
it denies the couple the opportunity to grow into their identities
together. By the time both have learned to be established and independent, they are set in their ways, and the necessary adjustments
to marriage can be more difficult to make. Sometimes these adjustments lead older, more independent couples into difficulty.

A young, naïve couple goes into marriage knowing there will
be challenges and adjustments that they are not really prepared to
make. Both partners know they are not adequate to make decisions
on their own, so they work together and pray a lot. They realize that
they need to communicate and pray together as if it's their only hope
for survival. This is the best way to start a marriage, and a younger,

less established couple is more likely to take this approach. They do not think they know it all, and they are not surprised when the fact is proven.

Remember, no matter how old or young you are, you need the Lord's help. You need to humble yourself continually and pray constantly. Don't assume you'll be more prepared later, and don't focus on the past as if your chances are gone. Just stay humble and continually work on becoming better. You're not trying to become the most eligible bachelor or bachelorette. You're trying to become the best potential eternal companion.

NOTES

1. Holland, "Some Things We Have Learned—Together."
2. Hinckley, "Living Worthy of the Girl You Will Someday Marry," 49.
3. John Bytheway, "I Have No Friends," *New Era*, Jun. 1998, 203.
4. Holland, "How Do I Love Thee?"
5. Thomas S. Monson, "Priesthood Power," 66–69.

eighteen

If Your Dating Efforts Just Aren't Working

I f you have made diligent effort, and still aren't having success, don't give up. If you are seriously trying, keep trying. If you stop, it may be harder to start up again later. Your lack of success doesn't mean you're not good enough for marriage. But it could mean there are some options you haven't considered yet.

ARE YOU BEING TOO PICKY?

Ugh. I'm sure you've heard this one plenty—and I'm sure you've wondered this about yourself. How do you know if you're being too picky?

Look at your top five list. If you don't have one, make one, and be honest about it. Then analyze it. Pray about it. Make sure this list includes the five things that are *really* most important to you. Then, when you are confident that these are the five things that matter most to you, let the other things go. If "blonde and blue-eyed" would have been your sixth item, then let it go. Look carefully at the things that really matter. Don't ignore red flags—just be willing to widen your horizon a bit.

How? If you find that you have been subconsciously insisting that you *must* find a girl who enjoys athletics as much as you do, let that go. It's okay in a marriage to have different interests. While the things you have in common may help you connect and understand each other, your differences will allow you to complement each other and will make for a more dynamic and versatile companionship. That diversity will really come in handy as your children come to you someday with different interests.

If you have been subconsciously insisting on a tall husband, try dating a short guy. If you have always looked for a musician, try a computer geek. Be creative in expanding your options, while keeping the most important things a priority. You may find your new approach fun and refreshing.

It helps to know that physical attraction often comes after getting to know someone. If you are not sure whether a potential dating partner is sufficiently attractive, try having a couple good, open conversations with her, and then see what you think.

ANALYZE YOUR METHODS

Another thing you may want to look at is your method. If you find yourself doing the same three activities for each new person you date, or always saying the same things to ask someone out, try mixing things up a bit. It could be that you've gotten yourself into a rut (possibly to avoid the common stresses that come with dating). Be willing to step out of your comfort zone. Talk to friends to see what they do. Break down the dates you've had in the past to see which parts tend to go well and which don't. If there's always the same awkward silence as you drive your date home, try finding a good "end of the date" game to play, such as making up stories about the people in the nearby cars or seeing who can think of songs that have a specific word in them.

If you find yourself always doing entertainment-based dates, such as movies, bowling, or laser tag, try some more lifelike or casual dates. Remember that while dating should be fun, entertainment isn't the final goal. You're trying to get acquainted enough to find out if you want to spend eternity together. Make dinner together, take a walk, or read a book together. We'll talk more about date ideas in another chapter.

ANALYZE YOURSELF

Just a heads up, this is the tough one. If you've made considerable, repeated effort to find someone to marry with no result, then there may be something about you that is standing in the way. Don't get down on yourself. Don't hate yourself, and don't blame yourself. Square your shoulders, keep your chin high, and ask yourself if there is something about your manners that's turning others away.

President Spencer W. Kimball encouraged those who were ready to make the effort when he said:

> You might take a careful inventory of your habits, your speech, your appearance, your weight, . . . and your eccentricities, if you have them. Take each item and analyze it. What do you like in others? What personality traits please you in others? Are your dresses too short, too long, too revealing, too old-fashioned? Does your weight drive off possible suitors? Do you laugh raucously? Are you too selfish? Are you interested only in your own interests or do you project yourself into the lives of others? Do you have annoying mannerisms?
>
> Do you repeat old stories till they are threadbare? Are you too anxious or too disinterested? Can you make some sacrifices to be acceptable? Are you dull or are you too exuberant? Are you flashy or are you dis-interesting? What do you do to make yourself desirable? Do you overdo or underdo? Too much makeup or too little? Scrupulously clean both physically and morally?
>
> . . . What are your eccentricities, if any? I think nearly all people have some. If so, then go to work. Classify them, weigh them, corral them, and eliminate one at a time until you are a very normal person.[1]

Whew! Ouch, I know. Okay, just take a breath, give yourself some time to think about this quote. Don't mope; just think about it, and then only long enough to make a decision about what you're going to do. Then move forward with whatever changes are needed. You're not giving yourself a personality makeover—you're just cutting out some unattractive habits or traits, and it may take time. You don't have to stop dating in the meantime. In fact, if you are dating often, don't lose your momentum, because if you are able to eliminate or reduce the thing that's been standing in your way, you may find success faster than you think.

For Older Singles

If you don't have the opportunity to marry in your twenties or thirties, you may have a tendency to assume that your prospects are past—that you will never have the opportunity to marry in this life. Don't get discouraged. Your Heavenly Father knows your fears, and He will help if you will turn to Him regularly. Express heartfelt gratitude to Him for all He has done for you, and express your confidence in His promises.

Believe it or not, there are a few advantages to dating at a later stage of life. Don't tell the younger folks this (we don't want them holding back intentionally), but for most older people, dating is more comfortable. They have passed the stage where they get nervous to see their date, and though they still feel strong attraction, it's a less demanding attraction. What I mean by that is they don't get as annoyed by little things like a crooked part in the hair or bad clothing styles. They tend to be more forgiving of the little things that for whatever reason somehow bother younger singles. Even the "ick" factor with things like flabbiness or other bodily flaws are less of an issue.

Because of this, some older singles are able to find each other and connect more easily and comfortably. Some older folks who experienced both younger dating and older dating prefer older dating for some of these reasons.

Also, many older dating relationships lead to marriage sooner, partly because the couple doesn't feel the need for an elaborate wedding, and they already have a permanent place to live.

Prepare for Change

There are, of course, some challenges associated with getting married later in life, and being aware of those challenges can help the two of you work through them smoothly.

For one thing, since both people are past the primary ages of personal development, both the woman and the man have become quite set in their ways. They have gotten used to coming and going as they please, and having to answer to no one. They have both become comfortable being alone, and no longer need the validation of others to feel comfortable with their own personalities. While that is a good thing, it makes it easy to be stubborn when compromise and kindness are needed.

If you are in a stage of life where you're able to live completely independently, and you want to meet someone and get married, prepare yourself now for change. Be ready and willing to give up those parts of your life that will be affected when you get married. Having this mental readiness will help you make the adjustment from singlehood to marriedhood much easier.

Often someone is an older single because they have been married before. Through divorce or death, many older singles have children already. That brings on a whole separate discussion, but I think it's enough to say here that it's important to be aware of the situation, and to be loving and sensitive to everyone involved.

Remember that marriage isn't just about you. It's mostly about selflessly caring for another person, and when children are involved, it's about selflessly caring for a whole family. There still needs to be wisdom, prayer, and honest communication with the person before considering marriage, but remember that family is all about service. If you join the family with a desire to love and serve, you'll have a great marriage and family.

No matter how old you are, never give up on your hope for an eternal marriage. Marriage is a beautiful thing in every stage of life, and there's no reason you should assume that your chance has past. Keep working at it, and you'll get there!

NOTE

1. *The Teachings of Spencer W. Kimball*, 295–96.

nineteen

~~~

Controlling Emotion

Paul H. Dunn said:

> If, in your case, the physical tends to dominate, all the more reason to bridle it and find the other dimensions. Bridle is the word that wise father Alma used in counseling his son Shiblon, and the promise he attached is the key to understanding: "Bridle ... your passions, that ye may be filled with love." (Alma 38:12.) Bridling increases strength, increases power, increases love. There are absolutely two ways you can control a horse. (We learned a little bit about horses last night.) One is to kill it; one is to bridle it. Alma never said kill your passions. The implication is not that passions are evil, that we shouldn't have them. On the contrary, we bridle something we love, something whose power we respect.
>
> A horse is stronger than a man, so the man bridles it, thus controlling its power and using that power for good. Passions are stronger than we are, so we bridle them, thus controlling their power and using that power to strengthen a marriage and forge it into eternity. One has to know how to bridle a horse or a passion.
>
> Remember, a physical relationship is simply too beautiful to squander, too wonderful to waste. It is the sterling silver too precious to tarnish before the beauty of the banquet.[1]

As a teenager, I remember having a remarkable ability to influence my own opinions. I distinctly remember being amazed at how

I could make conscious effort to like or dislike something, and it would be so. This was useful when it came to foods. There were a few foods I didn't like, but if I decided I wanted to like them, I could do it. It took some effort, but it worked.

I found that it also worked with hobbies and how I used my leisure time. I had a hard time reading scriptures at first, but I decided I would make myself like doing it. Just like with food, it worked. Of course, with spiritual things, I had the help of the Holy Ghost to influence my attitude, but it was a change nonetheless, and a powerful one.

I used this to develop an interest LDS contemporary music. I used it to develop interests in the hobbies of those I respected or admired. For example, I always looked up to my older brother Shane, who had a great interest in computers. I likewise wanted to be good at computers and developed a great interest in simple computer programming that lasted a few years.

Eventually I learned that this ability worked with people too. I could develop respect for people I knew I should look up to, such as my Sunday School teachers and the bishop—and even some of my teachers at school. Even with girls, I found that with time and effort, I could develop a crush. Strange as that may sound, it worked.

Once I figured this out, I found it easy to take interest in girls who had the values and personality I liked. Looks came along as I *decided* to take interest in them. I also found that I could use similar effort to destroy a crush. This was more challenging, since there were chemical and hormonal influences, and it took longer and used more effort, but it most certainly worked.

Once I fully realized what power I had to influence my own desires and interests, I looked back on my life and realized that for most of my life I had been making preference decisions, but I had been making them subconsciously. I had a sixth grade teacher— probably the best grade school teacher I'd had—who loved new age music. At the time I decided that I liked new age music too. Little did I know that this simple subconscious choice would lead me to someday publish my own new age albums.

For a long time, I thought I was unique: that my ability to shape my own desires and interests was a gift. But the more I observed and spoke to others about it, the more I concluded that my gift wasn't unique at all. During the teenage years, the mind goes through a period of growing and developing that makes it more moldable than at any later phase of life. This phase generally continues into the twenties.

Though I can still exercise this power, it's much harder than it was when I was a teenager. For some, this molding is done subconsciously, so they don't notice when their inappropriate or unwise decisions are changing their opinions and molding their minds to become something they don't intend to become.

That's why it's so dangerous to get involved with *anything* that can drive away testimony, spirit, and faith. You may unknowingly shape your own character into a form you don't want.

What does this mean for relationships and falling in love? Can a person actually decide who he is and isn't going to be attracted to? The simple answer is yes, no, and sometimes. What it really means is that we *can* mold our opinions *after* our first impression. Perhaps the first time I see a girl, I find her attractive. I then have a choice: I can feed the attraction, or I can ignore it. I can choose to pursue the attraction by thinking about and trying to talk to the girl, or I can choose to ignore the attraction and convince myself that I am not attracted to her. The latter is more difficult, but it is one of the most useful tools in dating and marriage. It takes work, but it's possible. You may not be able to control your initial first impression of a person, but you can control later impressions if you choose to do so.

When you experience a broken heart, you can use this knowledge to tear your heart from the person who hurt you. It's painful and takes time, but it's possible. If you deeply admire and respect a friend you don't find particularly attractive but who you know would be a good marriage prospect, you can use it to build deeper feelings. Lasting relationships can begin from this exercise.

Why would you want to do this? If you experience love (or

annoyance) at first sight, why would you want to shape your emotions against that first impression?

First, it can save you from great heartache and sorrow when interest in the wrong type of person could damage your spirit. Second, it can empower you to seek out the best possible companion. The fact is, most marriages don't start with love at first sight. Not all marriages even began with *attraction* at first sight. Most start with acquaintanceship, perhaps even friendship, which later develops a hint of chemistry. Then someone makes some kind of remark that hints in this direction. Eventually one asks the other out.

Sometimes feelings aren't reciprocated until time and shared experiences work their magic. After that, interest continues to increase until both are madly in love with each another. It can work!

Your ability to choose is more powerful than your feelings. You may not always be able to choose how you feel, but you can always choose how you will act. If you choose to do things that will feed love, you will develop stronger feelings of love. If you choose to do things that will starve love, you will lose feelings of love.

If you are dating someone you know you wouldn't marry, and you're struggling to know what to do, ask yourself if you have been choosing actions that feed love or starve love. If you're honest with yourself and find that you have been choosing to love this person despite your better judgment, then perhaps it's time to consciously change your choice. Say it to yourself, "I choose not to love this person." Say it out loud. Say it over and over until you won't forget your decision. Then *act* on that choice.

Does this make the feelings of love go away quickly? No. Does it mean you're fighting your emotions? Yes. But you must understand that you *do* have the choice whether to love this person. When you choose to *not* love them, or to stop feeding love, your actions will lead your feelings away from love just as they first led you *into* love.

I do not suggest that this is not painful. It can be torturously painful. Just remember that your power of choice is stronger and more powerful than your emotions. Agency will overpower the depth of your initial feelings. The pain will gradually subside until it is gone. The pain dissipates as the choice to love is starved. Your choices are greater than your emotions. Your agency is mightier than your feelings.

ANGER

One of the fastest ways to lose control of your emotions is through anger. Learn now to control anger because if you don't, it will control you. No one deserves to be married to someone who regularly loses his temper. Also, learn to be loyal to those you love no matter what you're feeling. Feelings cannot dominate your relationships, so the sooner you learn to control them, the better.

Jeffrey R. Holland said:

> You can't be a good wife or a good husband or a good roommate or a good Christian just when you "feel well." A student once walked into the office of Harvard Dean LeBaron Russell Briggs and said he hadn't done his assignment because he hadn't felt well. Looking the student piercingly in the eye, Dean Briggs said, "Mr. Smith, I think in time you may perhaps find that most of the work in the world is done by people who aren't feeling very well." . . . Of course, some days are going to be more difficult than others, but if you leave the escape hatch in the airplane open because you think even before takeoff you may want to bail out in midflight, then I can promise you it's going to be a pretty chilly trip less than fifteen minutes after leaving the ground. Close the door, strap on those seat belts, and give it full throttle. That's the only way to make a marriage fly.[2]

NOTES

1. Paul H. Dunn, "Teach 'the Why,' " *Ensign*, Nov. 1981, 71.
2. Holland, "Some Things We Have Learned— Together."

twenty

~

Same-Gender Attraction

The power to influence your own emotions is most effective in the teenage years, though it usually continues into the young adult years. Unfortunately, with the trends of the world, many young people are unconsciously using this power to confuse their own feelings. When a teenager has friends who have same-gender attraction, he may question his own feelings. "Am I that way, too?"

With all the anxiety and fear that comes as a natural part of the dating experience, a person may erroneously conclude that his heart leans another direction. Anxiety and fear of girls does not suggest he may not be interested in them. It actually says the opposite—the heart recognizes that if it follows its natural inclinations, it is about to face severe stress. In addition, many young people's interest in the opposite sex does not fully mount until the late teenage years. Many who experience this anxiety in their early teenage years assume they are actually attracted to their own gender, when the real issue is that their bodies simply have not completed puberty.

If, therefore, one is beginning to question his feelings about the opposite sex, he should be patient. He should use this power to mold his own emotions to prepare the way for the natural opposite-sex attraction that will certainly come in time.

Never forget the power of the Atonement of Jesus Christ. He

experienced everything. *Everything.* There is no sin, pain, inclination, weakness, or imperfection that He did not pay for through the Atonement. All the natural laws of justice and mortality were placed in His hands when He paid the price for all of them. Not only can He forgive us of our sins, not only can He help us become better, but He can even change the shape of our minds, hearts, and thought patterns. He can mold us into *anything*, but He will never do anything without our willingness to turn to Him for help.

If I have suffered a horrible breakup and I turn to Him for help, He can help me to reshape my heart to lose all feeling for the person that hurt me. If I feel the inclination to act in ways that I know would lead me to a place I know I shouldn't be, He can change the very thoughts that lead me to think about it. Never—*never*—underestimate the power of the Atonement. There is not one thing that the Atonement cannot do for a person who is willing to follow the Savior and turn to Him for help.

He can heal the broken heart, He can heal the homosexual, He can heal the child abuser, He can heal the fearful, and He can even heal the single adult. Does that mean He can make an undesirable person into an attractive person whom others would want to date? Absolutely. Can He really remove the mortifying fear that prevents some people from ever approaching the opposite sex? Certainly.

These things may take time and patience, but we ought never to doubt the Savior's capacity to make us into what we need to be. The key is to become and remain worthy and have complete and absolute faith in His promises. I know of no counsel given more times in scripture than "Ask, and ye shall receive" (see Matthew 21:22).

Some say that it is not fair to suggest that same-gender attraction needs healing, because, as they claim, it is a natural inclination. Whether or not a person is born with that inclination is irrelevant. Same-gender marriage is not available in the celestial kingdom. We have many natural inclinations that we can't deal with alone. Since the natural man is an enemy to God, we need God's help to overcome *all* the tendencies that prevent us from becoming like Him.

Elder Wickman said:

> Same-gender attraction did not exist in the pre-earth life and neither will it exist in the next life. It is a circumstance that for whatever reason or reasons seems to apply right now in mortality, in this nano-second of our eternal existence.
>
> The good news for somebody who is struggling with same-gender attraction is this: 1) It is that "I'm not stuck with it forever." It's just now. Admittedly, for each one of us, it's hard to look beyond the "now" sometimes. But nonetheless, if you see mortality as now, it's only during this season. 2) If I can keep myself worthy here, if I can be true to gospel commandments, if I can keep covenants that I have made, the blessings of exaltation and eternal life that Heavenly Father holds out to all of His children apply to me. Every blessing— including eternal marriage—is and will be mine in due course.[1]

Certainly we should tolerant of others and treat everyone with respect and kindness. We don't need to shun people who have a different sexual orientation than we do, but in terms of the legal and political battles dealing with the definitions of family, make sure you always stand on the Lord's side of the line. He knows more than we do, and in our efforts to help those who are gay, lesbian, transgender, and so on, let's be kind without forgetting that the Lord's way is always the kindest and most correct way, no matter what the world thinks.

And how do we know what the Lord thinks? It's very simple— the prophet will let us know. If you don't know what the prophet has said on an issue, find out. It's not hard, especially with all the resources we have now. Be willing to seek his words out, and courageous enough to stand with the prophet, whatever he says on the issue. Then get on your knees and pray for the courage to do what he says. Where the Lord commands, the Lord provides a way. If you promise Him that you will do His will no matter what, you'll be surprised at the power He gives you to resist the world's ideas and temptations.

In any sensitive or controversial topic, never forget Elder James E. Talmage's counsel: "We should look upon this body as something that shall endure in the resurrected state, beyond the grave, something to be kept pure and holy. Be not afraid of soiling its hands; be not afraid of scars that may come to it if won in earnest effort, or [won] in honest fight, . . . but beware of the wounds of battles in which you have been fighting on the wrong side."[2]

WHY I DO NOT SUPPORT GAY MARRIAGE

This life is not the beginning of our existence, and death is not the end of it. In fact, this life is a very short part of our eternal existence.

It is an eternal principle that a family consists of a man and a woman with their children. It is also an eternal principle that every man has always been a man, and every woman has always been a woman. Likewise, every man will always be a man, and every woman will always be a woman.

The few occasions where there is a physical defect in which a baby is born with either no sexual organs or both male and female organs does not change the eternal identity of that child, which includes his or her gender.

Gender is part of our eternal identity, and according to eternal principles, marriage is to be between a man and a woman. No other combination is a marriage in the eternal sense, and therefore no other combination can last forever. No matter what the government decrees, that eternal principle will not change.

For those who live a life in accordance with eternal principles, a simple mortal marriage is the seed that grows into an eternal marriage in the next life. No other seed will grow into an eternal marriage. There is no way for it to happen. Just as a pebble planted and watered cannot grow, a marriage between two people of the same gender cannot grow into an eternal marriage and will end with death.

The sad part about this is that those who are in such marriages do not realize that the result of their choice is only suffering. Part of that suffering will come when they realize that what they once thought of as an inborn part of their identity was only a mortal challenge that ends with death.

Many people think their tendencies are part of their very being, and ever will be. They think their attraction to their own gender is part of who they are.

Certainly such tendencies have a great impact on these individuals. Certainly these tendencies lead to almost unbearable longings that seem like they can only be relieved by either sin or death. Certainly this trial can seem insurmountable.

But this life is not intended to be easy. Our trials help us realize the extent of our potential. We will never know how strong we are until we face our biggest challenges and overcome them.

The agency and choices of the individual are stronger than life itself with *all* its inherent challenges.

Someone who faces the trial of same-gender attraction faces a difficult trial—perhaps even comparable to the trials faced by someone who is quadriplegic, or someone who has lost every person that they ever cared for, or someone living on the streets with mental illness.

Thankfully, God has provided a way that all of these people, by living faithful to His commandments and enduring their trials well, can, in the next life, receive every blessing denied them in this short life. For those who are truly faithful to God, these blessings will be accompanied by more and greater blessings than they can now imagine. No suffering in this life will not be well compensated for in the next life if we simply are willing to follow the commandments of God.

Some feel that God will accept them the way that they are and that He will love them and bless them with all the blessings He has to offer regardless of who they marry. But God doesn't break His own laws. He teaches eternal, unchanging principles and allows His children to choose to follow them. He even allows them whether or not to believe in these principles. But He does not remove the eternal consequences of those choices.

To anyone anywhere who is in a same gender relationship, I plead with you: consider the eternal nature of life. Consider the way you see things now is not the way you will *always* see things. The way you feel now is not the way you'll *always* feel. You may have tendencies and attraction toward people of your gender. You do not have to act on those feelings. Know that in time, if only in the next life, those feelings will pass, and if you have followed the Lord's commandments, the true and eternal nature of attraction will return to you. That may seem impossible to you now, but it's true. Your power of choice is stronger than your tendencies.

I'm not suggesting you marry someone of the opposite gender in hopes you will someday be attracted to your spouse. I'm suggesting that you stay close to the Lord. He will be with you. If you stay close to Him, He will guide you and give you all the help you need.

If my desire to save people from suffering can be called intolerant, so be it. If it's bigotry to make an effort to support laws that some day even the protesters will be grateful for, I guess I'm a bigot. But I won't just look the other way while people hurt themselves. And in this case, those who try to redefine marriage may also be hurting generations to come.

NOTES

1. "Same-Gender Attraction." The Church of Jesus Christ of Latter-day Saints Newsroom, 2006, http://newsroom.lds.org/official-statement/same-gender-attraction.
2. James E. Talmage, Conference Report, October 1913, 117.

twenty-one

The Digital "Meet" Market

D allin H. Oaks said:

> The best way to avoid divorce from an unfaithful, abusive, or unsupportive spouse is to avoid marriage to such a person. If you wish to marry well, inquire well. Associations through "hanging out" or exchanging information on the Internet are not a sufficient basis for marriage. There should be dating, followed by careful and thoughtful and thorough courtship. There should be ample opportunities to experience the prospective spouse's behavior in a variety of circumstances.[1]

If you are considering online dating, here are a few things you may want to think about before you get started. While online dating used to be considered a highway to trouble, it has since gained wider acceptance and has gotten many good couples together. Trends also show that with the passing of time, it will become even more popular. While you probably shouldn't use this as you primary source for finding dates, it does have value, and I won't discourage you from trying it. If you feel no desire to date online, don't do it. It's really only for those who feel confident with its potential and are ready to do the homework necessary to make it work.

NOT FOR MINORS

If you are under eighteen, don't even attempt online dating of any kind. The danger for you is too great, and predators can be terribly convincing. If you chat online, make sure it is only with people you already know in real life.

DON'T DATE ONLINE

To the rest of you, I want to stress this point: do NOT *date* online.

Wait . . . isn't this chapter about how to date online? It is. Let me explain. *Meet* online, then date in real life. It really should be called Internet *meeting*, instead of Internet *dating*. The idea is to get on a date. Obviously, you'll want to make sure the other person isn't a nutcase or predator, but once you have corresponded enough to recognize that he is a good person, meet him in person as soon as possible. There's a number of reasons for this. First of all, if you end up getting attached to someone you've never met, it's going to be heartbreaking when you learn that he is different than you thought. You may also find that you *are* attracted to them, and you may feel obligated to continue the relationship even if he is scum. If you meet *before* becoming attached, there is no relationship to continue, so breaking it off is a lot easier.

DON'T DATE OUT OF STATE

You may be tempted to date for a long time online if the other person lives out of state or far enough away that your schedules won't allow you to date in real life. This will inevitably lead to a breaking point that can become a real problem. You want to be with him, so do you move to his city, or does he move to yours? Do you wait for a commitment of a lasting relationship so your move doesn't waste time and energy? If you do, you're committing to a relationship with someone you don't know as well as you think you do. Don't become attached to someone before meeting him in person. If you do, you're setting yourself up for danger, or at least heartbreak. The easiest way to avoid this is to meet as soon as possible.

If you do end up dating someone who is close enough to date occasionally, but schedules make it hard to meet more than every couple weeks, consider doing video Internet calls, so you can still talk face-to-face.

NON-NEGOTIABLES

It's important that you have high standards when looking for dates online. Have at least three non-negotiables—three criteria that *must* be met by potential dates in order for you to even consider meeting them. You can do more if you choose—but if you do ten, it's going to be difficult to find someone. Still . . . have at least three.

I would highly, *highly*, suggest that one of those non-negotiables is having *current* temple recommend. If the person doesn't have one, he is not worthy to go to the temple, and you don't want someone like that. You're looking for an eternal companion, not a mortal buddy. Remember that by knowingly choosing to marry someone who is not temple worthy, you are knowingly forfeiting those eternal blessings. Be *sure* he has a temple recommend. And don't assume that just because his profile claims he has one that he does. Ask the person directly. If he thinks that's too bold or that you are being judgmental, then you don't want to date him anyway. You want someone who is excited to get married in the temple and who will insist that *you* must be temple worthy before he will consider dating you! You want an Abraham and Sarah marriage.

In light of that, don't go for a date who is looking for that special someone to get him back onto the straight and narrow. The Internet abounds with people who think they need someone who will help them back into full activity and full fellowship. Don't even consider someone like that. If he's not living the gospel now, he needs to fix that *before* looking for someone to marry. You want someone with whom you can be *equally* yoked, not someone who will expect you to do all the effort for the whole family in religious matters. That's way too much to expect of you, and it would be a difficult marriage.

DO YOUR HOMEWORK

Before diving into an online dating site, do some research. Talk to friends. Find out what others recommend. You can also do this by using Google searches to see what other strong LDS married couples recommend. Forums and blogs will have lots of advice about the best site. Don't just settle for the first one you hear about. If you see some that look good, try Googling the name with the term "scam," "avoid," or "don't use" next to it. People who have had bad experiences with a site will blab all over about it, making it easy for you to avoid similar problems. You may want to use more than one site, just so you can compare, but don't use too many or they'll become too much to maintain.

PROFILING

When you create a profile, be open, honest, and real. Don't make it sound like you are a doctor if you have just entered medical school, and don't lie about anything or give people the wrong impression. Don't give personal information that could make it easy for you to be found in real life by psychos. You don't need your address or phone number on your profile. You can give someone your phone number *after* you have been in contact with him directly by messaging or email.

Make sure your picture is a good representation of you. Don't use a photo of yourself making a goofy-face or snuggling your dog (unless of course you are naturally goofy faced or constantly rolling around with your dog). Also, don't use a professional glamour shot. It may be attractive, but it's not the real you.

You may want to have a trusted friends or family members look at your profile to give you honest feedback about whether it accurately represents you. If they have recommendations, consider what they suggest. If they say you are being too humble, try to open up and be honest. If they say you are exaggerating or being too fake, try to tone it down and be honest.

NOT A SHORTCUT

One of the biggest mistakes people make with online dating is that they think it will get them results faster. The truth is, it takes just as much work, effort, and emotional trauma to find someone through the Internet as it does to find someone through any other means. Don't have unrealistic expectations, and don't assume that because you have agreed to meet, that it's going to work. Try to think of it as, "Let's meet, just in case something might come of it." Then if it doesn't work, it's not a big deal.

AVOIDING TROUBLE

Beware of wolves in sheep's clothing. Use your instincts, listen to the Spirit, and follow your hunches. Remember that with the Internet, anyone can post anything almost anywhere. The picture may be of a young, good-looking guy, but he may be either using an old picture or one he found on Flickr. If you find that the person you are emailing has a tendency to hide information, stop the contact and don't pursue him further. Another clue is when someone posts lewd pictures on his profile. Any inappropriate pictures posted on a profile or sent to you (by email, phone, or message) means that person is a trap. Period. End of story.

Once you begin communicating with someone specific, don't email back and forth and back and forth. Contact each other enough times to establish that you're both basically trustworthy, and then meet. If the person is not willing to meet, don't pursue him any further. Break it off now. If he isn't ready to meet, he is a waste of time and emotional energy. A good rule of thumb is to meet within a month of your first contact.

If you find someone that interests you, you can contact him directly (by email, or messaging, or whatever)—in this field no gender roles exist of who should contact whom first. If he doesn't reply the first time, feel free to send him a second message. But don't contact him more than twice if he doesn't respond. If he's on vacation, he'll respond when he returns. If he doesn't, it means he's not interested.

When you decide to talk in person, and if you're nervous about giving your phone number, sign up for a Google voice account or similar service. You can call or receive calls from any phone, and their caller ID will see it as the Google number instead of your home or cell number. You can block numbers as well if necessary.

LET'S MEET!

When you do agree to meet your date, choose somewhere public. Encourage a simple activity that will be short, maybe an hour, so you can break the ice without too much stress. That will give you a chance to find out if your date's profile is accurate, and if it goes well, it will leave you both wanting more time together. (Hint to girls: some lower life-forms think watching a movie is license to get all physical . . . just a heads up.)

Rather than having him pick you up, meet at a public place you've agreed on. This is a basic safety precaution and should be standard for a first date. If it goes well, and your date is worth pursuing, you can give out your personal information and allow him pick you up on the second date. If you'd rather meet somewhere again for your second date, that's fine too. Until you've been on a few dates, always tell a trusted friend or family member where you will be and who you are meeting. Don't just go without letting anyone know. Remember, whatever he says on the Internet, he's still a stranger until you meet in person.

Try to be yourself. Be open and honest in your conversation. Ask direct questions that will save you stress and time, such as, "Do you have a temple recommend?" If your date bent the truth on his profile or let his profile get out of date, you need to know, and he's more likely to be honest face-to-face.

If you find someone online, when do you take down your profile? The simple answer? After you've had the talk and decided together that you aren't going to date other people

After you've exchanged personal information, such as phone numbers and addresses, it's always a good idea to introduce your date to the family and meet your date's family. Whatever he may have said online, you will learn a lot about your date by the way he treats family.

DON'T SAVE SERIOUS TALK FOR EMAIL

Once you've met and are dating regularly, you are no longer "dating online." You're just dating! So try to use your face-to-face time wisely. *Don't* save the serious conversations for email unless you both have decided that's the easiest way for you to communicate openly. If things aren't working out, don't drop him an email and say you're no longer interested (unless it's only after the first date—that's early enough, I suppose). If you decide it's time for the talk, don't have it over email or chat. Remember that if things work out, you'll have to talk about serious things face-to-face, so the sooner you can learn to do that, the better. Once you do, you'll find it *much* more satisfying and thorough than email or any other form of indirect communication.

It helps to consider that when you are talking face-to-face, both of you are exercising your "best self" skills. If you tell your date something is bothering you, he'll react in his best-self mode, and he'll try hard to understand. With email, however, all guards are down. Your date may swear at the computer and then respond more brutally than he would have while under the filter of kindness. And if he misunderstands, he's going to fume about it for a while before having the issue cleared up. In person, you can clear up issues before any conclusions are drawn.

NOTE

1. Dallin H. Oaks, "Divorce," *Ensign*, May 2007, 70–73.

twenty-two

~~~

Dating Ideas

My intent in suggesting a bunch of dating ideas is not to tell you what dates work best but to get your mind thinking in terms of what *kind* of date would be best for a particular situation. If your date is shy and quiet, for example, you probably don't want to take her to do karaoke, but it would be good to do something that would help get your date talking, in order to get to know each other better.

Do you need to know your date's stand on an issue but don't know how to ask? Are you struggling to find things to do that you *both* enjoy? Do you find it hard to keep conversations alive and vibrant?

Perhaps it's not that the relationship isn't working but just a sign you need to try a different kind of activity in order to explore all sides of your relationship. Here's a list of dates that might help generate your own date ideas to meet the needs of your growing relationship.

TRADITIONAL DATES

Sure, they may not be original ideas, but they've been popular for so long for a reason. While some may get bored of these if done too often, these classics are always an option and are almost always fun!

Movies. Make sure it's a decent one. Cheesy or boring is not too big a deal, but at least make sure the movie you choose doesn't go against your values—and even more important, make sure it doesn't go against your *date's* values. If you want to quickly lose your chance with a good, faithful Church member, just go to a movie that makes her feel uncomfortable! For Jenni and I, the best movies live up to our standards 100 percent *and* provoke good conversation. It's fun to see a great movie and then spend the rest of the date talking about it. The more interesting, funny, thought-provoking, or meaningful the movie is, the better this works. But if nothing else, an old Disney show is fun to see too. If you find yourself in a movie that does not live up to your standards, don't stay. You'll destroy your chances with this person if you do, but you'll score big points if you turn and say, "I'm sorry. I didn't know it would be like this. Maybe we should leave." If by some chance your date is somehow offended by your request, then perhaps this person is not the best match for you anyway. I also repeat my warning that some guys (lesser guys) think watching a movie automatically gives them license to get all physical. Ladies, he shouldn't get physical before you are ready, so you may want to bring it up beforehand if you're going to a movie. If he doesn't respect your desires and gets physical anyway, drop him immediately.

Dinner. This may seem like a risk-free date, and it can be, as long as you do the most basic communication with your date. But if you assume too much, you may get into unnecessary trouble. If you ask someone on a date, don't just say, "Where would you like to eat?" But rather something like, "What is your favorite kind of food?" or "Are you a Mexican or Italian fan?" Or you could try asking something like, "I was thinking we could eat at either Denny's or Olive Garden. Which sounds better to you?" That will prevent your date from feeling pressured to eat Italian when they are sick of it, since they don't have the nerve to say, "*Anything* but Italian!" If your date still doesn't want to decide, then just pick one. Don't *make* her decide, but if possible, give options.

Bowling, mini golf, laser tag, corn mazes, and so on. These dates are almost always fun and require no skill at all. In fact, in my experience, the less skill you have, the better. The secret to making these activities fun is to really get into it. Don't just go through the motions like you don't want to be there. Try adding some rules, use silly names (where applicable), and be willing to laugh and make it fun for your date. Jenni and I like to use what we call "Calvinball" rules. Basically you make up new rules for each turn and never play the same way twice. "Okay, every time the ball hits more than two walls on one turn, you have to shout, "Yeeehaw! I win!" The sillier the rules, the more fun it will be.

Concerts or plays. These can be anything from pop artists to symphonies. Just remember the same rules as with movies. Never take a date to a concert where the music challenges the values held by you or your date. It's better to go to a terribly dull concert than a fun, low-standard concert. Basically, if the lyrics or dress of the artists do not meet Church standards, don't go. And just like with a movie, if you discover partway through that this is the case, just turn to your date and say, "Do you mind if we leave?" That will leave a better impression on your date than if you had gone to a fantastic show and thoroughly enjoyed it.

Ice-Breaker Dates

Sometimes the hardest part of going out with someone is just penetrating the shell of awkwardness that is inherent in first (and sometimes second) dates. Here are some ideas that might help both of you feel more relaxed and have a great time.

Do a group date. They're not just for teenagers, and it's easier to keep conversation alive in a group. If you really want to help your date feel comfortable, plan a double date. Have a friend of yours ask out your date's friend, and then go do something as a group. With her friend there, your date will be more likely to act natural and have fun. If you don't want to line people up, just plan a group date of three or four couples. If you get enough good people together for a fun activity, everyone is likely to have a great time.

Go to a mall, museum, zoo, or gallery. If you walk around a mall or gallery together, there's a lot to see and a lot to spark conversation. Zoos and museums have a lot to see, hear, and explore. Anyplace with displays of different kinds will provide dozens of avenues for conversation. If conversation starts, don't rush through it to get to the next display. Instead, use the opportunity to learn about your date and to help her get comfortable talking with you. The conversations that you have will do more for nurturing a potential relationship than anything else.

Do something athletic, such as a sport, together. Even something as simple as Frisbee can be a lot of fun on a date. If you are both decent at a certain sport, play it together. Sometimes doing something physically active can help both of you get your mind off the fact that you're on a date. When your body or mind is active and focused, your emotions are generally positive, and your experience together will likely be uplifting and fun.

Anything you can do that will get both of you laughing—(a funny movie, a clean comedy show, whatever it may be.) Humor breaks ice faster than almost anything.

CREATIVE DATES

If you or your date is the creative type, then doing a date that will bring out your creative side not only allows you to learn more about each other but gives an otherwise quiet person an opportunity to shine a little. Creativity doesn't demand a lot of extra preparation—just a little, well, creativity!

The Story Game. This one requires a group of at least four people and can include any number beyond that. Give everyone a piece of ruled (lined) paper and fold it three ways so there is a top, middle, and bottom section. Have everyone write the beginning of a story in the top line and fold that section out of sight. When everyone's ready, pass your paper to the right and have everyone write the end of a story (just a random story, not the end that matches their beginning) on the bottom third of the paper. When everyone is done with that, pass it again and allow everyone to silently read the beginning and end of the story and fill in the middle section of the story to make the beginning and the end flow. When everyone is done, pass their papers one more time to have everyone read the stories out loud. We've found this to be an absolutely hilarious game and very fun.

Progressive picture or cartoon. Give everyone a piece of blank printer paper to draw a cartoon. Then pass it to the person next to them so they can add something. Keep it going around and around for as long as the group wants. You would think this would be a quiet game, but it is actually loud and funny.

Sing a duet or quartet. If one of you can play the piano or guitar, sing together. Since you are not performing, you don't have to worry about sounding perfect. Just have fun together. If you both play instruments, consider having a little jam session.

Charade dancing. If you both enjoy dancing, go to a dance where there will be upbeat group dancing going on. Then, instead of doing traditional dances, act stuff out! You wouldn't believe how much the repeated motion of "vacuuming the floor" can look like a real dance! Try driving a car, putting on a jacket, or dribbling a basketball. Challenge each other with different actions and have a contest to see who can come up with the coolest or most authentic-looking dance.

Paint together. Start with a fresh canvas or paper and paint!

Sculpt. Get some clay, or if you must, play dough, and sculpt. You can get oven-bake clay from any craft store, and if you do, get some acrylic paints to decorate your creations.

If it's Easter, decorate eggs. If it's near Christmas, get some craft stuff to make tree ornaments. If it's near Halloween, make costumes together. If it's near Valentines' Day, make Valentine boxes like you did in elementary school. Whatever holiday it is, make something together for it.

Act. Play a type of acting charades where one person acts and talks like a famous person. The other person asks open-ended questions and tries to guess who his date is pretending to be. Questions like "What is your life philosophy?" or "What is your favorite type of food?" can lead to funny and lively responses.

Origami. Get a library book about origami, and do origami together. But only use the book at first. Try to create paper foldings of your own making. If that sounds like a bit much, try inventing a new kind of paper airplane. You wouldn't believe how much fun it can be to fly paper airplanes on a date!

Hairdo. Take turns giving each other new hairdos. Get some combs, brushes, gel, hair spray, or whatever else you need, and style each other's hair.

GET-TO-KNOW-YOU DATES:

One of the most important parts of dating is getting to know your date. Whether you're going on a first date with this person, or you just want to better know and understand your boyfriend or girlfriend, here are a few date ideas that might help you get to know your date better. These still work great even after you're married.

What's Your Favorite Smarty? My family and I made up a game a few years ago that we call "What's Your Favorite Smarty?" In this group game, you come up with a question, such as, "What is your favorite food?" or "What is the thing that frightens you more than anything else?" Someone is designated as being it, and then the players write on a piece of paper what they think that person would answer. The person who is it writes down his own answer. Then everyone takes turns reading their answers, and then finally the one who is it answers the question. Whoever was closest to that answer wins the round. It's really a lot of fun, and you learn a great deal about everyone who is playing.

Walking or hiking. Taking a walk or hike can take the awkwardness out of silences, making it easy to think about what to say before you start a conversation or change a subject. The longer the walk, the more likely your conversation will lead to learning new things about each other.

Read a book together. This works really well with nonfiction, such as Church magazines, personality-type books like *The Five Love Languages* or *The Color Code*. If there is a topic that interests both of you, get a book on it and read it together on a date. Jenni and I found that one of our favorite dates was making a picnic or popping corn and going to a park to read a book together. We just take turns per page and have a great time doing it. You can do it with fiction too, but nonfiction will get you talking about real things, such as values, philosophy, current events, and psychology. Doing so will not only help you learn about your date, but you may learn a few interesting things about yourself.

Board and card games. A number of board and card games encourage talking and sharing opinions. They can be as silly as *Would You Rather?* or as detailed as *Truth or Dare.* Find a game that will encourage getting to know each other better.

FUNNY DATES

Make a video. I know of no way to make a serious video. The more serious I try to make it, the funnier it turns out. If you don't feel creative enough to come up with a plot, just make a spoof on a favorite movie. I once did a group date where we made *The Princess Bride.* I think we played two or three roles each. Another time, we did *One Bride for Seven Brothers.* It doesn't take acting skills, just a sense of humor. Oh, and don't forget to make commercials.

Goofiest thing in the store. Go to a store—any kind of store—and give each other five minutes to find the weirdest or funniest thing in the store. If it's a group date, go in couples. Otherwise, just separate and come together again in five minutes. Did you know that at an ordinary grocery store you can get pickled watermelon rinds? Yeah . . . we've played that game a lot.

Bubbles. Go to a toy store and get some everlasting bubbles and blow them in a public place. Malls, fairs, parks, and even colleges are great places to fill the air with bubbles. If you can't find everlasting bubbles, regular bubbles work too. Everlasting bubbles won't pop, so they stick around a long time, and they also travel far. Regular bubbles are cleaner, though, so if you are somewhere with lots of cars or windows, it's best to stick with the ordinary type. You can blow them out the window of your car—providing the driver isn't doing the blowing. Bubbles are a guaranteed smile from everyone who sees them, and you and your date will be laughing the whole time.

Get on YouTube and watch funny videos. They have *Americas Funniest Home Videos*, among others . . .

Calvinball (mentioned previously). If you've ever read the comic *Calvin and Hobbes*, you'll probably remember a game they played called "Calvinball." To this day I'm not clear on how it worked exactly, but there were two elements that were always consistent: they never played the same way twice, and they made up the rules as they went along. So whatever activity you're going to do, use Calvinball rules—make up new rules as you go along, and play it differently on each round. Maybe take turns making up rules each hole, or each turn, or whatever. For example, if you're playing mini golf, you can make a rule that every time the ball hits a wall, you have to cheer, or every time you hit the ball you have to hit it with a different part of the putter. Calvinball works with any activity with traditional rules; bowling, sports, pool, ping-pong, board games, card games, or even snowball fights.

Consider the needs of the person you're taking on a date. Consider the needs of your relationship. What type of date would help you discover more meaningful things about each other? What kind of dates will help your relationship progress?

You may want to consider making your own list of date ideas for future reference. Consider making lists for many different types of dates, such as:

Relaxing Dates

Educational Dates

Dates that Include Family

Athletic Dates

Spiritual Dates

Free Dates (these are especially good after marriage!)

Culinary Dates

Spontaneous Dates

Service Orientated Dates

Emotional Dates

Conversational Dates

Financial Dates

twenty-three

~~~~~~~~~~

Goals

One of the important lessons I had to learn quickly in dating is to not let fear of the future rule the present. I suppose I wasn't unique in wanting to get just the right girl on the first try. As a teenager, I used to think to myself: *Wouldn't it be cool if the first girl I ever have two dates with turns out to be my wife?* Well, that goal was spoiled in high school when a girl I asked out asked me to a school dance, and we never went out again.

So I modified my goal: *Wouldn't it be cool if the first girl I went out with twice—where I did the asking both times, was the girl I ended up marrying?* Well, shortly after my mission I went on a blind date with a girl, and it went well. I thought I might kind of like her, so I asked her out again. That didn't last, although we did go on a total of three dates.

So I modified my goal again: *Maybe the first girl I go on more than three dates with will be my wife someday.* Well, a year or two after my mission, I met a girl who I liked, who liked me, and we hit it off okay at first—we even decided after "the talk" (we'll discuss what "the talk" is later), that we would consider each other boyfriend and girlfriend. A couple weeks later, we broke it off.

So much for my goals. I hadn't yet held hands, kissed a girl, or fallen in love, so I thought about forming new goals around those things. But after that last failure, those kinds of goals suddenly seemed silly. The point was not to succeed without failure; the point was to succeed at all. I was looking for an eternal companion, and if that meant first holding hands with or falling in love with a number of girls I wouldn't end up marrying, so be it. The Lord never said I had to get it right on my first try.

In fact, I think there is benefit in dating a good number of girls. If in that process you find one that you think just might have a slight chance of being the one for you, don't be afraid to encourage things to progress that way. That's how relationships are formed. Once you find someone that meets your basic requirements, it will likely take risk and commitment to learn about the deeper aspects of the person's life. You aren't likely to find out a person's dirt or gems on the basis of simple friendship. And once you do get close enough and make simple commitments to each other, you'll find out more about your date than you could in casual dating.

You need to learn as much as you appropriately can about a person before deciding to marry them. You won't learn everything before marriage, but the more you learn, the more equipped you are to make that decision.

One day I attended a fireside talk by John Bytheway. His topic was "What I Wish I'd Known When I Was Single." The whole talk was basically about single life and the dating game. One of the things he mentioned was that in his search for a wife, there came a time that he decided he would go on a date at least once a week.

I thought a lot about that resolution. By this time in my life, I had slowed my dating progress and was going out about once a month but still didn't feel like I was getting much accomplished in the dating game. So I made a similar resolution (though not as intense): I would ask a girl on a date at least every other week. That was my rule.

For me, this was a very effective plan. For one thing, it got me going on dates more often, and going on dates provided the social and emotional development I needed to handle the whole dating experience. Of course, some of the early attempts at this program were rather humiliating, but with practice, asking girls on dates became far less traumatic.

Second, following this plan allowed me to focus on what I could control. My job was to ask a girl on a date. If she said "no," then I was off the hook for a couple weeks. It never does any good for anyone to focus on what he or she can't control. I could only improve myself and try again with a different girl later. I'd try to give myself a better hairstyle or wear a different deodorant. I'd try working out a bit more and cutting back on my bad habits.

This pattern of every other week dating (and it wasn't too long before I was going on dates almost every week) turned out to be one of the most fun periods of my life. I learned a lot and met a lot of great people. Though it could be frustrating when these efforts didn't seem to lead to any serious relationships, I was learning how to interact with girls and learning what to look for in a girl—and what to look out for.

twenty-four

The Talk

In every dating relationship, there comes a time when the two must decide where things are going—they talk about their feelings for each other, what to do about them, and whether they should commit to dating exclusively. This is not marriage proposal, and it's not a promise of an eventual marriage proposal. It's just an opportunity to talk openly enough so that she knows where he stands, and he knows where she stands.

Sometimes the talk results in an exclusive relationship, and sometimes it results in a breakup. Both outcomes are stressful, but sooner or later, every couple must have the talk. For some this may be a sentence or two, and for others it may be a four-hour conversation. But for most, it's just long enough to share feelings and make commitments. Sometimes it merely results in a decision to keep dating while taking things slow. The purpose of having the talk is not so much about the result as it is about breaking the wall that stands between the two of you, so you both know what is actually going on in each other's mind and heart. Many call this, "defining the relationship." It's the point where all that pent-up energy expended on weighing signs, wallowing in self-consciousness, and stressing about what the other person is feeling is released into open, honest communication.

Most couples have dated each other at least a few times before having the talk. Some have dated for months before having it. It really depends on the individuals. Often it's initiated by the first one who feels confident about his or her feelings (whether for moving forward or breaking up). Technically, ending the dating relationship is not considered a breakup before the couple has the talk, since you really don't know how each other feel before you talk about it.

It's Not as Scary as It Sounds

To a person who has never experienced the talk, it sounds terrifying. Don't worry. Just as with other aspects of progressing in a relationship, you are more prepared for it than you think. You have been equipped with the emotional power to communicate openly, and once the talk begins, you'll be amazed at how liberating it is. Once the conversation starts (getting up the courage to start the talk is the scary part—just like the courage to ask someone out is the scariest part of the date), your heart will free up and your communication will be better than it's ever been with this person.

If the Talk Results in Commitment

So what do you do if the talk results in a commitment? Well, that mostly depends on the commitments you make. What kinds of things should you decide? That will also vary for each couple, but there are some common elements in most "talks."

You will probably discuss whether the two of you will date steadily and exclusively. You might want to talk about physical boundaries—making a conscious decision together regarding how far you will and will not go physically. For some, that may mean you will decide not to even hold hands yet, and for others, it may mean you won't let your kisses get too involved. But whatever you discuss, it's good to promise each other that you will keep the law of chastity under all circumstances. Making this promise protects you both from that temptation, and makes it easier to live the commandment.

You may also want to discuss ways to have more open discussions, such as a bi-weekly stroll or dinner that is set aside just for talking about the relationship. This prospect will only sound scary to those who have not yet had the talk. Having that initial talk opens doors to communication in ways you may not have thought possible. Now that the communication walls are broken, you will feel freer to talk about things more openly more often. Be open and honest. Don't constantly nag your partner about how the relationship is going, though that ought to be discussed fairly regularly also. But use the opportunity to learn deeper things about each other, such as dreams, goals, values, and even things such as where she hopes to live someday and what child raising ideas she intends to use.

Obviously, you shouldn't feel obligated to talk about marriage yet, but it wouldn't be a bad idea to talk about it in a general way, such as talking about relationship advice that you've heard or things that you hope to do similar or different than your parents someday. These kinds of discussions can help the two of you begin to shape what kind of relationship you want to have, and that shaping will be crucial if you do end up marrying this person.

When you have the talk, do it in person. You really can't have the talk by email, since you can't see the other person's body language or hear their intonations. If you can't do it in person, at *least* do it by phone, not by texting or Internet chat. They need to hear the inflections in your voice. Besides, you're practicing relationship skills in hopes of getting married someday. You can't have serious talks with your spouse by email. The sooner you learn to really talk, the better prepared you will be for marital communication.

twenty-five

~~~~~

Breaking Up Is
Hard to Do

There are countless reasons for breaking up, and whether they seem like legitimate reasons or not, a breakup is still a breakup. If you know that the person you are dating is not the kind of person you should marry, then it is your responsibility to break it off.

Jeffrey R. Holland said:

> In a dating and courtship relationship, I would not have you spend five minutes with someone who belittles you, who is constantly critical of you, who is cruel at your expense and may even call it humor. Life is tough enough without having the person who is supposed to love you leading the assault on your self-esteem, your sense of dignity, your confidence, and your joy. In this person's care you deserve to feel physically safe and emotionally secure.[1]

But even when the reasons for the breakup are not due to faults in one or both people, breakups are usually painful for at least one of the two.

One possible sign that a relationship is not working is if your feelings of obligation are stronger than your feelings of interest. While there is always going to be a sense of duty and a desire to please, if you find yourself wishing you didn't have to call, didn't have to go out, or didn't have to bring your date, these are good signs that you should break things off. There will always be a strong sense of loyalty once you have become serious in your relationship, but if you find that you don't have the desire to please her, then something is going wrong. For example, if every time the person calls, you find yourself dreading answering the phone, it means the relationship is not working.

Some couples use physical affection as a substitute for whatever is lacking in the relationship. After all, even though they don't know each other, kissing still feels good, and cuddling still makes them feel loved. This mistake could be morally dangerous and prevent the opportunity to find a more fulfilling and lasting relationship with someone else. Physical affection should branch out of respect, friendship, and a desire to provide love and comfort, not as a substitute for those things.

Once you know that things aren't going to work between you, it's much kinder to break it off immediately than to wait and hurt the person even more later. If you make the mistake of continuing even after all hopes for the relationship have past, you may begin to resent and avoid the other person. Rather than manipulate and find excuses for your negative feelings, consider that perhaps the relationship ought to end. The best thing to do is break things off and find someone with whom you *can* be happy to try to please.

When you decide that the relationship is over, break it off quickly and clearly. Don't draw it out over a month by starving the person of your attention. While it may still hurt, breaking up will save the other person a month of suffering that could have been used for healing and seeking a new relationship instead.

Remember too that no matter why things didn't work, you can and should forgive the person. There's no reason to continually blame him for his faults or your broken heart. Things didn't work out. That's all. Don't overlook problems, and don't allow yourself to stay with or return to a relationship that can't work. But you can forgive the person and move on. Grudges, bitterness, and gossip only hurt you and your opportunity for future prospects.

WHEN THE TALK RESULTS IN BREAKUP

What if the talk results in a breakup? What then? That really depends on which side of the breakup you are on and *why* you broke up. While some breakups are a result of a mutual feeling that things aren't going to work out, most are initiated by one of the two of you.

For the Dumper

If you are the one who breaks it off, and you're quite sure you don't want the relationship to lead to marriage, then you need to back off. Don't try the "let's just be friends" thing. It rarely works. And if by some chance it *does* work out, it will be because the one you hurt initiates it. Only the other person should make the attempt. If she does, welcome the friendship, recognize that you will never be as close as you once were, and be careful not to lead her on to think that she has another chance at being your partner—unless you become absolutely sure that's what you want. Otherwise you need to give her space. If she was really interested in you, she is hurting. You will feel tempted to comfort her. That's not your place, and the attempt will only hurt her more. Don't call her and don't visit her. Don't avoid her, but don't seek her out. If she wants to talk or maintain friendship, she will come to you.

BYU psychology professor M. Gawain Wells said:

> If your dating relationship feels joyous and healthy, if both of you feel the Lord's approval of your decision to marry, then the relationship "works," and you marry. If it doesn't work, you don't marry. There is no third alternative.
>
> However, many people assume there is a third alternative and try to keep the relationship alive when all signs of vitality have ceased. Both in my Church callings and in my profession as a clinical psychologist, I have worked with people who cannot accept breaking up as a healthy part of the selection process of courtship. Instead, they see it as a time to punish themselves, to feel hurt, or even to try to hurt others.[2]

For the Dumpee

If you are the victim in a breakup, and you had really hoped things would work out, you are going to hurt. What do you do first? Get yourself an ice cream cone or a goodie. Don't try to eat away your troubles, just get something small to soften the initial impact. It doesn't have to sink in all at once. Then, if you need to cry, do it. For some people, tears cleanse the heart of anger. It hurts, so don't expect to blow off high hopes as fast as the person blew you off. It took you time to learn to really care about this person, and it will take time to lose those feelings. Take it a day at a time.

Don't *blame* yourself. That's useless, and it only leads to depression. Learn from the experience, change anything specific that you know you need to change, but know that you will be changing for some other future prospect, not for the person who dumped you. You can remain friends if you choose, but don't expect to win him back. If you feel that there is something of fault on your part, give yourself ample recovery time before thinking much about it, and, even then, use what you learned to do better the next time. There is an old saying that I think applies well here, "The wrong one is the right one to lead you to the best one."

If you use these trials to learn and grow, and not let discouragement overtake you, you will one day find someone else whom you learn to love more than the person who dumped you.

Try not to take out your frustrations on your family, friends, or the opposite gender at large. Not only does it cause you and them unnecessary extra hurt, but it can burn bridges to future prospects. Most people don't want to date someone who handles breakups badly. Even Jenni and I wouldn't have gotten married if we hadn't both handled our own breakup well. That was one of the things that impressed me about Jenni—she was still kind to me, even after we broke up for awhile. Because of that, it was a lot easier for me to beg her forgiveness and start over with her.

DON'T BIND YOURSELF TO A DATING FAST

Another word of advice to the dumpee. I have a motto (I have many mottoes) that can apply to nearly any situation: don't make decisions on a rush of emotion. If you're feelings are fired up, you're not in a state to make decisions. If you really feel the need to decide something, just write down the idea, but don't commit to it yet.

For example, don't decide that you're going to wait six months before dating again. If you feel that you need some time, tell yourself that you need time, but don't set a time frame. You will heal faster than you think, and getting back into the dating game can help with that healing. If you have committed to six months of date-fasting and you meet a fabulous prospect during that time who you would love to learn more about, your commitment will not help you to pursue this person. Take time if you must, but don't set a time frame.

On the other hand, if months are passing, and you still have no desire to start back into the game, you may need to set a goal for yourself to begin dating again within a month or two. Setting proactive goals can help a lot.

Bruce C. Hafen said: "Avoid the habit of feeling sorry for yourself, and don't worry excessively about those times when you feel socially unsuccessful. Everybody in the world doesn't have to marry you—it only takes one."[3]

DON'T FORGET THE POWER OF AGENCY

If someone dumps you, you may be tempted to feel that this person was the love of your life, that no one is like him—that you could never love another like you love this person. Is there any hope for you? Will the hurt ever end? Will that love ever go away?

Unrequited love is a great struggle for one who is seeking an eternal companion, and even for a few who have somehow resigned themselves to a life of loneliness.

Some mistakenly think that they have fallen for someone so deeply that they will never truly love another like they do that person. They think that if there is no way to win that person's love, then they are doomed to a life where they will have to be alone or settle for a second or third choice. They assume that though they may learn to love someone else, it will never be as deep as the love they had for the other.

What these individuals forget is that just as we have a choice to love, we have a choice *not* to love. This may sound simplistic, but it's true. It takes time, and it takes a great deal of energy, but who we love is a choice, and it is a choice that *must* be made by those who experience unrequited love if they are ever to find a truer, more lasting love.

One of the keys to choosing not to love is to realize that it takes just as much (sometimes more) time and energy to fall out of love as it does to fall in love. We cannot expect to walk away from being dumped and be instantly healed. Healing takes time and energy. But this means more than just letting go of our feelings.

PARABLE OF THE BEAUTIFUL CITY

Imagine you are driving down a beautiful road headed for a city that you really want to reach. But before you arrive, some traffic police motion you off the road and say, "The road is closed. The city gates will not open until next season. You cannot proceed further." You can see the city in the distance. It looks beautiful, and you want to go, but you know that there is no way to get there. In vain you beg the policeman to make an exception.

Likely, you will sit and consider your loss for a time, but soon you will have to turn and go back or seek a different destination. Finally you get in the car and turn the steering wheel, but you don't go anywhere. No matter how hard you turn the wheel, you remain where you are. What's wrong?

You must accelerate. You have to move. Of course you must turn away, but until you *accelerate* away, you will never leave. The city will forever be in your view until you leave. If you do accelerate and consistently drive another direction, you will eventually be out of sight of the city, and if you're persistent, you will find an even more beautiful city.

There's nothing proactive about wallowing in the pity of unrequited love. Of course there is a time of mourning. It's a painful time, but when the initial shock has past, you must accelerate away from that loss. So how do you do it?

Decide to *Not* Love

First, you must make the choice to leave. Deciding to leave means more than accepting the fact that you will never win this person over. This means deciding to do what's necessary to stop loving this person. You must choose *not* to love, and then work toward fulfilling that decision.

Don't Look in Your Rearview Mirror

Every time you look at the person's photos, love notes, or drive slowly by the person's house, you renew the feelings of love and loss, and you are only re-deciding to love the person. If you truly want to get over the person (and there will be a temptation to *not* get over them), remember that you are only delaying better opportunities that may be just out of your present view.

Keep the Car at a High Speed

Don't slow down your life. In fact, speed it up. Get busy doing things with family, friends (sans your ex), hobbies, exercise, talents, and projects. Don't let too much spare time be wasted thinking about the past, and *never* let yourself get bored. Boredom is a strong catalyst to counterproductive thoughts and emotions.

Keep an Eye Out for Other Cities

This may seem to some like running from pain, but when you are getting over someone, you have a powerful ability to show and build love. This is partly because unrequited love increases your sensitivity to loving actions and emotions. If you choose *not* to love the one you lost and choose *instead* to love someone else that you find, you will find that not only can you love this new person completely, but your feelings for the other person will diminish considerably.

Many people may caution you to not rush into another relationship, and if you have not already accelerated away from your last love, they are probably right. You cannot seek someone just to save you from your pain. You must not consider using someone to make your past love jealous. You also must make sure that this new person meets all of the necessary criteria to be a good potential spouse. But if you have been making a sincere attempt to lose your feelings for your past love and are determined to find someone better, then you can proceed confidently, focusing all of your attention on the growing new relationship.

Choosing Not to Love

One of the most underestimated powers in the universe is the power of agency. It is this power that has brought about every good thing in our lives. This power distinguishes us from all other forms of life. But we often treat is as though we don't have it at all.

We often refer to love as something we fall into, even by accident, as if helpless. But the fact is, choice is the greatest factor in determining who you fall in love with.

You *choose* who you will love. Once you do, you then act on the choice you have made. As you choose to act on your choice, emotional connection will take place. That connection will increase as you feed it with more actions. After a time, you will feel that twitterpated feeling. That feeling is what most people call being "in love."

Lynn G. Robbins said:

> Somewhere in the history of the English language the expression "fall in love" began to be used to describe the sublime experience of finding someone to love. While it is a beautiful idiom, there was inherent risk involved in selecting the verb *fall* because it mostly means accidental, involuntary, with no choice involved. And subtly, it has also led to the use of its distressing corollary, "We fell out of love," an all-too-common phrase heard nowadays as an excuse for a failed marriage. "Falling in love" and "falling out of love" sound as if love were something that cannot be controlled.
>
> . . . There are no perfect marriages in the world because there are no perfect people. But our doctrine teaches us how to nurture our marriages toward perfection and how to keep the romance in them along the way. No one need ever "fall out of love." Falling out of love is a cunning myth which causes many broken hearts and homes.[4]

You may forget that you have been making choices all along. At any point you could have chosen to stop doing those actions that lead to love. But once you have chosen to do those actions, and once they blossom into love, you no longer have a choice to not be in love. That choice was already made—whether consciously or not.

You do still have choice, however, about what you will do with the love, or feeling of love, that you have. You can continue to feed it, or you can kill it. You do either by choosing your actions and your attitude.

NOTES

1. Holland, "How Do I Love Thee?"
2. Wells, "Breaking Up without Going to Pieces: When Dating Doesn't End in Marriage," 58.
3. Hafen, "The Gospel and Romantic Love," 10.
4. Lynn G. Robbins, "Agency and Love in Marriage," *Ensign*, Oct. 2000, 16.

twenty-six

Brother or Sister "Right"

"The fulness of eternal salvation is a family matter."[1]

Jeffrey R. Holland said: "If you are just going for pizza or to play a set of tennis, go with anyone who will provide good, clean fun. But if you are serious, or planning to be serious, please find someone who brings out the best in you and is not envious of your success. Find someone who suffers when you suffer and who finds his or her happiness in your own."[2]

There are a number of things you should consider while trying to find a spouse, but there is one thing that tells more about a person than any other of which I am aware. It is simply worthiness. If you are serious about wanting to marry for eternity, I would suggest that you not even go out with someone if you know they do not have a current temple recommend. And even if they *have* one, don't even consider going out with someone if you know they are not worthy of the recommend they hold.

Some may say, "Oh, but he is such a good person . . ." as if saying this can change his worthiness. If he's not worthy, he cannot marry you in the temple. And if he is not worthy to marry you in the temple *now,* then you must assume that he never will be worthy, no matter how seriously he's trying to change.

We've already discussed that it is unfair and unwise to consider that a prospective spouse will change in the future. You need someone who is ready and worthy *now*. If he insists that he's working his way back, tell him he can always come looking for you again *after* he has a recommend. If he considers you judgmental for this, then he doesn't know the seriousness of his situation. If he does accept and understand this, he may be back later, and you can date him *then*. This applies to both genders.

Why do we so adamantly insist on a temple wedding?

Here's a really dorky parable to illustrate what I'm talking about:

> Once there was a man who saved all his money and went on a three-day cruise. He'd always wanted to go on a cruise, and the cost to him was well worth the sacrifice. The first day was spent in learning, exploring, and becoming familiar with the ship. The second day he began to meet people, and even met a wonderful, beautiful woman of his age at a dinner party—and for both of them, it was a case of love at first sight. After the date, they agreed to spend the next day together.
>
> They indeed spent the whole third day together. They ate meals together, they explored together, talked, danced, walked the deck together, and when night came, they observed the stars together. So happy were the two, so in love, that they pledged to one another to make the evening last forever. Hand in hand, they talked well into the evening.
>
> But sadly, the evening did come to an end. The ship quieted, the lights went out, and the two separated back to their rooms. Both slept restlessly, longing to be with the other.
>
> By morning, the cruise was over, and both went back to their homes. Since no contact information had been exchanged, they never saw each other again.

What a tragedy! Why would two people who really love each other allow this to happen? Yet, often it happens in the Church. We have access to the power that makes a marriage last forever. Just like the three days on the ship, our lives pass so terribly quickly. Avoiding temple marriage is like neglecting to share contact information on the cruise. When it's over, we'll go our separate ways if we don't have the relationship sealed by the hand of God.

As members of The Church of Jesus Christ of Latter-day Saints, we hold the most wonderful news in the world. We have opportunities available to no one else. Among these blessings is the possibility to get married in such a way that our relationship can last forever. This is not a metaphor. This is not wishful thinking. It is fact. Marriage can last forever. It's *intended* to last forever.

In fact, it is *only* through the gospel of Jesus Christ that this blessing is possible. There is no eternal marriage outside of the Lord's plan. To suppose that there might be some other way to be together is wishful thinking.

That is why the greatest decision you will ever make in this life is who you marry.

Bruce C. Hafen said:

> Don't date someone you already know you would not ever want to marry. If you should fall in love with someone you shouldn't marry, you can't expect the Lord to guide you away from that person after you are already emotionally committed. It is difficult enough to tune your spiritual receiver to the whisperings of heaven without jamming up the channel with the loud thunder of romantic emotion. The key to spiritual guidance is found in one word: worthiness. I won't take time to discuss it now but would urge you, if you want to do a little scripture study, to compare Doctrine and Covenants 63:16–17 with Doctrine and Covenants 121:45–46. You'll find something interesting there. Those who garnish their thoughts with virtue have the Spirit and have confidence in God's presence. Those who have lust in their hearts can't have the Spirit.[3]

Anything short of eternal is of no lasting value. Our spirits are eternal. Our ability to think and feel is eternal. Our value has eternal potential. How could anyone willingly submit to a marriage that carries no promise of eternal permanence? Relationships are only of real value if they have the potential of lasting forever.

Spencer W. Kimball counseled: "Clearly, right marriage begins with right dating. . . . Therefore, this warning comes with great emphasis. Do not take the chance of dating nonmembers, or members who are untrained and faithless. [You] may say, 'Oh I do not intend to marry this person. It is just a "fun" date.' But one cannot afford to take a chance on falling in love with someone who may never accept the gospel."⁴

Families are forever. That is a promise, but it is a promise that we must *choose* to take part in for it to be fulfilled. With few exceptions, all families will last forever. So what are the exceptions? Some will choose not to marry in the temple, and some will not live faithful to the eternal covenants made in the temple. All others will be eternal. Is that an exaggeration? No. Families will be forever. The only ones who will not be part of an eternal family are those who choose not to be sealed for eternity and who do not remain faithful to covenants.

President Hinckley has said, "You will wish to be married in one place and one place only. That is the house of the Lord. You cannot give to your companion a greater gift than that of marriage in God's holy house, under the protective wing of the sealing covenant of eternal marriage. There is no adequate substitute for it. There should be no other way for you."⁵

Why is it that some members of the Church, knowing the doctrine of eternal families, choose to reject the doctrine and marry outside the temple? There may be a number of reasons.

One reason is they may not have a firm testimony of the truthfulness of the gospel of Jesus Christ.

Another reason is that they may feel that because of past mistakes and inadequacies, they do not feel worthy of the blessing. To them I would remind that God wants you to succeed even more than you do. Have faith in his promises. Have faith in the Atonement of Jesus Christ. It is real.

A third possible reason—and perhaps the most common reason—is that they fear that they will have only this opportunity to marry. Better to marry outside the temple than not marry at all, right? Wrong. Better to try and fail than to willingly choose to fail when things get tough. Remember that God has promised that all who worthily seek the opportunity to marry in the temple, but do not have the opportunity in this life, will have those blessings after they die. Those who knowingly and willingly marry outside the temple do not have this promise. In fact, to them is given the warning that if they do not change their hearts and marry under the Lord's covenant, they cannot be together forever.

You may struggle with feelings of self-worth—most of us do, and not just during our adolescent years. But if you really truly know that you are a child of God, then you know that your worth is infinite and your potential is limitless. Such a being, especially one determined to live up to his or her potential, is not only worth marrying but is a great catch!

Elder Angel Abrea said:

> God is the actual father of the spiritual bodies possessed at that time. This is not a case of creation but of procreation. Brother B. H. Roberts explained:
>
> "I call attention to this distinction that when in our literature we say 'God created the spirits of men,' it is understood that they were 'begotten.' We mean 'generation,' not 'creation.' Intelligences, which are eternal, uncreated, self-existent beings, are begotten spirits and these afterwards begotten men. When intelligences are 'begotten' spirits they are of the nature of him who begets them—sons of God, and con-substantial with their Father." . . .
>
> So when we make reference to members of mankind as sons and daughters of God, it is not a symbolic term. Our Heavenly Father is the actual father of the spiritual bodies of mankind.
>
> We have been begotten and born of heavenly parents; God is our Eternal Father, the Father of us all. In consequence, we are his children, and therefore we belong to his family. Since we are to become like him, "perfect, even as your Father which is in heaven" (Matthew 5:48), family life is vital for Latter-day Saints.[6]

God is our Eternal Father. For eternity, we will be His children. His children will grow to be like Him (except for those who choose otherwise) and will have eternal families of their own. Eternal family is the rule. It is the norm. It is the eternal plan of happiness to which we all have access. The only ones who will not be part of the plan are those who choose some other course. *They* are the exception.

Will you be the exception? Will you choose to marry outside the temple? Will you risk eternal life on the remote chance that your partner might change his or her mind and live the gospel someday in the future? Choice is the most powerful influence we have. Will we waste it on poor decisions? Emotion is powerful, but it's not as powerful as choice. You may be in love. You may be *madly* in love, but if you know that marrying this person would be a poor choice, you must allow decision to overrule your emotions. Why? Because choosing to marry someone who cannot take you to the temple cuts you off from the ability to have your family last for eternity.

Your family ties could be cut off forever if you make an unwise choice—remember that God honors our decisions, wise or foolish.

I am speaking to those who knowingly marry someone who might never accept the gospel. For those who have no say in the matter, the Lord prepares all blessings for those who are faithful according to what they have.

So let's say you are madly in love with a person, and she with you, and you realize that this person cannot or will not take you to the temple—you can't be sealed to them. You know you must break it off, however painful that will be for you.

Small decisions almost always have big results. We rarely take note of them in the moment. It's usually after an accumulation of many small decisions that we make the large "closing" decision. That's the decision that usually gets the credit. But the fact is, big decisions are merely the outcome of dozens of small, seemingly insignificant decisions. The hardest type of small decisions is the one whose result you know could be big. This is often the case in dating. You must choose eternal life. Don't cut yourself short. You can try sending your partner to the missionaries, but if she's not interested in joining the Church, you must break it off. I know it sounds terribly unromantic, but you're not here to have a romantic experience. You're here to follow your Heavenly Father and become like Him. There is a good chance your partner will not understand, no matter how you tell her that it can't work between the two of you.

It is a small thing to ask a girl out. But the result could be eternal life-altering. That's one of the reasons dating is so frightening. Decide early to become serious with only someone who has a current temple recommend. I promise it will be worth it.

NOTES

1. Dallin H. Oaks, "Apostasy and Restoration," *Ensign*, May 1995, 87.
2. Holland, "How Do I Love Thee?"
3. Hafen, "The Gospel and Romantic Love," 10.
4. Kimball, *Miracle of Forgiveness*, 241–42.
5. Hinckley, "Living Worthy of the Girl You Will Someday Marry," 49.
6. Angel Abrea, "A Divine Nature and Destiny," in *Brigham Young University 1998–99 Speeches*, 15 Jun. 1999.

twenty-seven

~~~

Choose, But Choose Wisely

Sometimes while I was dating, I wished there was someone that could just show me the girl I would someday marry. I prayed for guidance, secretly hoping—sometimes almost desperately hoping— that the Lord would give me some kind of revelation to tell me exactly who I should marry. That would have been the easy way. I had given the Lord my life, my time, and all I would ever have, so why could He not do me this one courtesy? Wasn't this the most important decision of my eternal life? Why couldn't the God of the universe simply give me a clear answer when I asked, "Who should I marry?"

But I knew that wasn't His way. He had always guided and assisted me in the decisions I made, but I soon learned that when it came to *this* choice, I would only be allowed to ask permission. He would not tell me. He doesn't usually tell people *who* they should marry. We should not expect a revelation telling us who to marry. Even if we ask for one, we probably won't get it.

Bruce R. McConkie said:

> How do you choose a wife? I've heard a lot of young people from Brigham Young University and elsewhere say, "I've got to get a feeling of inspiration. I've got to get some revelation. I've got to fast and pray and get the Lord to manifest to me whom I should marry." Well, maybe it will be a little shock to you, but never in my life did

I ever ask the Lord whom I ought to marry. It never occurred to me to ask him. I went out and found the girl I wanted; she suited me; I evaluated and weighed the proposition, and it just seemed a hundred percent to me as though this ought to be. Now, if I'd done things perfectly, I'd have done some counseling with the Lord, which I didn't do; but all I did was pray to the Lord and ask for some guidance and direction in connection with the decision that I'd reached. A more perfect thing to have done would have been to counsel with him relative to the decision and get a spiritual confirmation that the conclusion, which I by my agency and faculties had arrived at, was the right one.[1]

There are rare exceptions. Some are given revelations of who they should marry, but such instances are rare enough that you can safely assume that it won't happen to you. If it does—well, then congratulations, your search is over.

If You Get a Revelation of Who to Marry

Incidentally, if you are so lucky, and the Lord gives you clear direction of who you should marry, *don't* tell the person who you are directed to marry about the revelation. Let the Lord give her the same revelation. Put the Lord to a test—if you're a guy, ask the girl to marry you; if you're a girl, get the guy to ask you to marry him. See if the revelation really was from God by going forward without telling the other person. It's not asking for a sign because Heavenly Father directed it. It's testing the Lord's promise.

Unless the Lord directs you otherwise (which I don't think He'd ever do), keep the revelation to yourself until *after* the other person accepts your marriage proposal. It's unrighteous dominion to announce your revelation before the other person has made her own choice. The revelation was for *you,* not the other person. They are not under your stewardship, and you don't have the keys to direct her life. If she needs a revelation in order to accept you, let the Lord do His own work.

If, after putting the revelation to the test, the relationship doesn't work out, then consider this statement by M. Gawain Wells:

Some couples may argue that they received a spiritual confirmation of their relationship. Why, then, didn't it work out? It's possible, of course, that you wanted so badly for it to work out that you misinterpreted spiritual feelings and, in essence, put words in God's mouth. But there's another possibility: People change. Though the dating relationship was right at one time, it isn't anymore. The spiritual confirmation could have been an assurance of the relationship's capacity, its possibility, its potential. But it wasn't a guarantee of ultimate fruit.[2]

GOD TRUSTS US ENOUGH TO CHOOSE FOR OURSELVES

Most people have to choose for themselves and then get confirmation from the Lord that their choice was good. Choosing an eternal companion with the Lord's help is one of the most exciting opportunities He has given us. For God to leave this decision in our hands is one of the greatest evidences we have of His love. He trusts us to be wise. He trusts us to seek direction from Him and to go forward according to our best judgment until we receive that direction. He has left that greatest decision up to us.

The Lord loved me enough to allow me to bumble through the process and learn what kind of companion I really wanted. He wanted me to search so hard that when I finally found a girl to spend eternity with, I would appreciate her more. He knew that I would love my wife most if I knew that I was the one who made the choice. I chose her, and she chose me. Ultimately, Jenni and I *became* soul mates, not because we were destined to come together, but because we chose to be.

Spencer W. Kimball advised, " 'Soul mates' are fiction and an illusion; and while every young man and young woman will seek with all diligence and prayerfulness to find a mate with whom life can be most compatible and beautiful, yet it is certain that almost any good man and any good woman can have happiness and a successful marriage if both are willing to pay the price."[3]

So when it came down to it, I would have to choose. *I* would have to be the one to choose. Not destiny, not fate, not even predestination in most cases. Even God would not make that decision for me. What a blessing! What a frightful burden! What a compliment and what trust. He will guide, He will correct, and He will let us know if we're going in the wrong direction, but He leaves the choice to us.

NOTES

1. McConkie, "Agency or Inspiration—Which?"
2. Wells, "Breaking Up without Going to Pieces: When Dating Doesn't End in Marriage," 58–61.
3. Spencer W. Kimball, "Oneness in Marriage," *Ensign*, Mar. 1977, 3.

twenty-eight

～～～

Loneliness

In searching for an eternal companion, a loneliness exists that is unlike any other kind of loneliness. It goes beyond longing. It is like a missing piece of the soul that your heart seeks in vain. It is not like grieving. Grieving carries the hope of reunion. It is not desperation. It's a loneliness unique to itself, and I think I felt it often during my single years.

Bruce C. Hafen said:

> There are times when we wonder if the Lord loves us; we wonder if other people love us. And so we mistakenly seek the symbols of success—whether that is being popular or being rich or being famous within our own sphere. Sometimes you may let someone take improper liberties with you, or you may indulge yourself in some practice that seems to bring temporary relief but only makes you feel worse in the long run. Some even make poor marriage choices, just to show the world that somebody will have them.
>
> Ultimately, however, only the Lord's approval of our lives really matters. If you seek to be worth knowing and seek to do his will, all the rest will take care of itself. Never forget that all things work together for good to them who love God (see Romans 8:28). Your time for marriage may not come until the autumn of your life and then, in Elder Packer's phrase: "be more precious for the waiting." Even if your time should not come in this life, the promises of eternal

love are still yours in the Lord's view of time if only you are faithful.[1]

While I was dating (in vain), loneliness abounded. I wasn't unhappy. It wasn't that I felt broken, but I did feel as though I was lacking something, and I knew what that something was. I knew I wouldn't feel completely whole without an eternal companion.

Patricia Holland said, "Please don't feel you are the only ones who have ever been fearful or vulnerable or alone—before marriage or after. Everyone has, and from time to time perhaps everyone will yet be."[2]

During my own years of loneliness, I would sometimes see two people pairing off at an activity—not to some inappropriate location, just to a more secluded area where they could talk more privately. When I happened to come across such couples, I could tell their conversation was deeper than I'd had with a girl, and I'd feel a twinge of jealousy.

It wasn't the people I was jealous of; rather, I envied the opportunity they had to share with each other so openly and exclusively. A similar feeling came over me at wedding receptions. I usually made effort go with others, so I'd have people to talk to and joke around with. But once in a while the reception was for a friend who didn't know any of my close friends or family.

Something about attending alone was a terribly lonely experience. There I'd be, watching the celebration of the union of two people. I wanted the same blessing. I wanted to have someone I could share everything with. I wanted to be someone's one and only. To see someone else succeeding at what I wanted more than anything always left me feeling a bit hollow. I was always happy for my friends—very happy for them—but the longing for the same blessing was terribly powerful.

I think other people are only vaguely aware when someone is feeling this way. Receptions, movies, empty Friday nights, or even just casual walks can feel terribly lonely.

Don't forget that the Savior is always there. Sheri Dew said:

There is Power in the Atonement of Jesus Christ. Until I was in my thirties, I thought the Atonement was basically for sinners—meaning that it allowed us to repent. But then I suffered a heartbreaking personal loss and began to learn that there was so much more to this sublime doctrine.

My solution initially to my heartbreak was to exercise so much faith that the Lord would have to give me what I wanted—which was a husband. Believe me, if fasting and prayer and temple attendance automatically resulted in a husband, I'd have one.

Well, the Lord hasn't even yet given me a husband; but He did heal my heart. And in doing so, He taught me that He not only paid the price for sin but compensated for all of the pain we experience in life. He taught me that because of His Atonement, we have access to His grace, or enabling power—power that frees us from sin; power to be healed emotionally, physically, and spiritually; power to "loose the bands of death" (Alma 7:12); power to turn weakness into strength (see Ether 12:27); and power to receive salvation through faith on His name (see Mosiah 3:19). It is because of the Atonement that, if we build our foundation on Christ, the devil can have no power over us (see Helaman 5:12).[3]

During this time of turmoil, I began praying harder about who I should marry. One night I was feeling particularly lonely, and I turned again to prayer. I told the Lord that I would marry whoever He suggested. I wanted it to be given to me. I wanted a clear response, if the Lord was willing to give it. So I asked. I begged. I pleaded to know who I should marry. I couldn't seem to get an answer. I kept at it.

The answer wasn't coming—but I did have a feeling that I should turn to the Book of Mormon for help. I flipped open my Book of Mormon aimlessly, and the page fell on Alma 30:44, where it says, "Thou hast had signs enough; will ye tempt your God?"

Puzzled and a little surprised at this, I thought back. Had I already received inspiration about who I should marry? Had He already told me? What signs had I received? I couldn't remember being told . . . then it came to me. I remembered the feeling I'd received long ago that the Lord wanted *me* to make the decision. As I returned to my knees and asked if this was the sign or inspiration I had already received, it was as if I audibly heard the words, *"You choose!"*

My first thought was of burden. Then humility. I had already been given an answer and had forgotten or doubted it for a while. I begged forgiveness and knew that the next time I came to ask about who to marry, it would be to ask for confirmation of *my* choice.

I began to realize that there was more to my search than choice of *who* to love. There is also the choice of who to *love*. It's not a matter of choosing a girl until she accepts a marriage proposal. You've got to make the choice to love her. Love is a choice. It is a choice as certainly as the choice of who to ask out or who to get to know. The only difference is that the choice to love carries enough emotional power to sway your power of reason. The choice to love is like the tiny cockpit of a massive airplane—it directs this immense structure that can carry hundreds of people to anywhere in the world. But the control panel itself is small, and the switches are few compared to the consequences of their use.

NOTES

1. Hafen, "The Gospel and Romantic Love," 10.
2. Holland, "Some Things We Have Learned — Together."
3. Sheri Dew, "You Were Born to Lead, You Were Born for Glory," in *Brigham Young University 2003–2004 Speeches*, 9 Dec. 2003.

twenty-nine

Rules for the Dating Game

I t makes sense that we would call dating a game because it involves so much strategy, skill, and luck. Think about it. A guy asks a girl out. Does he like her, or was she just a convenient choice at the time? She doesn't know. She accepts. Does she accept because she likes him or just to be nice? He doesn't know. He's late picking her up and gives a decent excuse. Is he trying to send the message that he is not taking the relationship seriously, or did he really have car trouble? She doesn't laugh at his joke. Is that because she's trying not to lead him on, or did she just not know it was supposed to be funny?

Then there's the whole timing thing. When does he put his arm around her shoulder? He doesn't know. When he does, is he really interested or is he too physical? She doesn't know. When does he tell her his feelings? If he tells them too soon, he may scare her off, but if he waits too long, she may lose interest or find a more interested guy. There's really no end to the guessing and risks that are possible in the dating game. There's also no way of knowing which girls like what when, or which guys will want what. It's exasperating!

One thing is for sure. We can't take ourselves too seriously in the game. Sure, a great deal is on the line, but everyone does stupid things, and everyone fails often to some degree. In fact, you only really can succeed at dating once. Anything short of a marriage that lasts your whole life can be considered a loss. You lose. Game over. At least that round is over. You can either marry and stay with your spouse. Or you can keep playing until you marry and stay with your spouse.

The only other option is to not play—which I don't recommend.

If only there was a rule book for the dating game, something to refer to in order to know what to do during any given play. Well, sorry, there's not, but as Jenni and I were dating, we discovered a few of the rules (though even these rules are not hard-set; they vary from person to person). Some of these rules are obvious, and others are completely based on a context. By the way, they are not in any order—other than the order of when we thought of them in making this list.

- At the end of a date, the guy should walk the girl to her front door.

- Never kiss on a first date—save that for when you are in love with each other. Hugs are usually okay, but if it seems awkward at the time to try to hug your date, a simple good night is always acceptable. (Never do a handshake—can we say, "Cheeseball"?)

- When you do kiss, keep it simple—a good rule of thumb is keep your mouth closed until you are married, even through the engagement. This may sound strict, but it helps both to avoid temptation and helps you keep perspective of why you chose this person. Don't worry, you'll have plenty of opportunity after you get married—that's when kissing gets really fun!

- If you are a guy and you're trying to decide whether the girl you want to ask out might be too young, just apply this simple equation: take your age and divide it in half. Then add seven. If she is that age or older, you're probably okay. You can ask her out. If she's younger, either find someone else or wait a few years until she fits that equation. For girls, reverse it. Your age minus seven, and then doubled—though I don't know of such an equation if the girl is older than the guy.

- Until you have the talk, both you and your date are free game and cannot expect the other to avoid dating others.

- Don't talk about past boyfriends or girlfriends on a date. It's just bad form.

- It's okay and good for a girl to ask a guy on a date, but after the first date, it should usually be the guy's responsibility to ask for a second date. However, once they have both asked each other out at least once, either can ask the other as many times as they want. But, guys, it's still primarily your responsibility.

- Every trustworthy person who is a member of the Church deserves a first date if he asks you out. This cannot be considered a commitment of any kind but is a common courtesy. After the first date, you should feel no obligation to accept another date if you don't want to.

- If the first date goes well, and the guy wants to ask the girl out again, he should contact her within a few days (usually about two days later but never more than a week later).

- To girls: if the guy has not called you within a week of your first date, you should (for your own sake) assume that he's not going to ask you out again.

- If you have gone out with a person three times and don't think you would really like to keep dating this person, it is your responsibility to turn the person down for the next date. If you don't, you will lead him or her on, and you are dooming them to a painful loss. If you are still not sure, feel free to keep dating, but don't keep dating if you know you're not interested. In short, it is your duty to turn a person down if you know after three dates that you will never marry them.

- Extravagant first dates rarely leave a good impression on the girl, but they always leave a deep impression on the wallet.

- The key to a good first date is planning something that is simple and fun.

- If you ask someone on a date and decide after the date that you don't want to go out again, you have no obligation to contact him or her, by phone or otherwise. If you do see him, treat him nicely, but don't feel obligated to ask him out again.

- Learn to handle breakups well. Don't blame the other person, and don't blame yourself. It just didn't work out. Learn from the breakup, and use what you learn to improve your skills, but blame no one.

- A movie is not a snuggle-fest. Don't treat it like one. In terms of physical affection, you will be more respected for what you withhold than for what you give.

- Once you've had the talk, be totally open and honest about everything, whether it is about your feelings, your goals, your fears, or your frustrations. Remember to *listen* first and talk second.

- First dates should just be fun—no serious relationship talks and no physical affection. Just have a great time together!

- While you'll probably have to be alone together for situations like driving and dropping off, don't linger in such situations too long. Being in public can help you avoid temptation.

- Always be kind—even if you have to break things off or say something that you know will hurt your date. Even bad news can be said kindly, and your date deserves your kindness.

- Don't gossip. Whether you're talking to your date about someone else or to someone else about your date, gossip can destroy lives. How can you tell if what you're saying is gossip? If you are speaking negatively about someone, ask yourself honestly if you're saying it in order to get advice, offer someone help, or protect someone's safety. If it's not for one of those reasons, it's gossip.

- Never ignore red flags. Take them seriously, and talk to someone trustworthy, such as parents, about them. If necessary, talk to your date about them. That will allow them to explain if you misunderstood. If your date tries to justify a red flag, see through the justification—recognize it for what it really is, and be prepared to break things off.

- While hints and signs can communicate a lot, they don't *count* for communication. Don't assume that because you send out a "vibe" that you don't like a person that he got the message. You need to talk. This isn't high school or television. A flirtatious glance can't take the place of the words, "Can I kiss you?"

- Always treat your date's family (especially parents) with respect. Also, always treat your own family with respect.

- Don't be hypocritical. Be yourself. If there is something flawed about your character that would turn dates off, change your character before asking someone out. This includes Church activity. If you're not worthy of a temple recommend but tell people you're going to marry in the temple, make sure you become worthy (and get a recommend) before going out with them.

WHERE TO MEET PEOPLE

For many, the question is not what to do once you're on a date, but how to get a date in the first place. That too can be a game, and a frustrating one. One thing to remember is that if you're not where the guys or girls are, you'll likely never meet someone. You can't wait at home and expect someone to call. Here is a list of some ideas of where you can go to meet someone.

College. Consider signing up for a class or two that there's likely to be many members of the opposite sex. If you're a guy, try home economics, foods, or music. If you're a girl, try sports, auto mechanics, or computers.

Institute. My top recommendation! I can think of no better way to find out someone's feelings about the gospel than at institute, where the spirit is strong and gospel discussion is active. In my experience (and I have a lot of institute experience), institute is much more interactive than seminary. Some just leaving seminary assume that institute is a dull substitution for seminary. Wrongo, bongo. Not only is the energy fun and spirit equal in every way, but the social game is a whole lot more active and productive. In institute, dating and mingling is encouraged much more than in seminary, and the activities are calculated to get people meeting. So go to institute, and GO TO THE ACTIVITIES!

YSA wards. They're really quite fun, actually. They've gotten a bit of a bad rap from certain films that have come out bearing the name, but believe it or not, they're generally quite enjoyable and comfortable. You'll probably get opportunities to serve in places where you wouldn't otherwise, since the whole ward is composed of young single adults. And the activities can be a lot of fun. The secret to attending a singles ward is to step just a little out of your comfort zone and try to reach out to others. Not only will this provide opportunities to serve and bless others, but you'll be noticed by members of the opposite sex.

Other options. Consider these other activities that can provide opportunities to meet and get to know other adults your age:
- Private schools (social dance, acting, choir, art, technology, sports, kung fu, community ed, and so on.)

- Appropriate online dating (See chapter 20)
- Community events
- Book clubs, health clubs, writing or music groups
- Volunteer
- Work (this is actually a very common place for people to meet)

The secret to meeting someone through one of these programs is to be *consistent*. If you're going to college, go to every class. If you're attending a singles ward, go every week and attend as many of the activities as you can. Guys often need to build up courage to ask girls out, and girls often need to build trust before they're willing to go on a date with a guy.

Exposure increases fondness, so the more you come, the more likely someone will take interest in you—unless, of course, you're a jerk, in which case you better change that first. If you're attending a class regularly, time will make you more attractive to those in the class. Don't be so immature as to assume that love at first sight is common or even realistic. If you're asked out by the perfect guy on the first meeting, you're rare indeed—and you probably don't need this book anyway. If you show up to an activity, find someone gorgeous, ask her out, find out she has a fantastic personality, and end up marrying her, you're the *exception*. That doesn't happen very often!

Besides, most people like to get to know at least a little about others before they go on a date with them. As you attend regularly, you will start catching people's eyes.

Also, don't stop at just attending. Even going to college, where there are lots of guys and girls in your classes, is not enough. The same with singles wards: just attending a singles ward probably won't get you on a date. It is important to attend the activities. If you're going to school, go to the special events and take advantage of extra-curricular opportunities.

It's at those kinds of events that you'll be able to interact socially with the people you have met in class or at work. When there's a work party, go to it. If there's not a party, host one. Suggest to your social dance class that you all go get ice cream after class. Interacting in a less structured, more personable situation will open up doors to conversation that would never have come through the regular routine. Those kinds of things will increase your opportunities for dates more than you may know.

Your intent in hanging out with singles is to get dates. So my only warning about that is if many months go by of regular hanging out, and nothing is happening, move on to a more productive venue. Find one that gets you on dates.

For me, attending these type of functions fueled my dating life. First, it provided opportunities for me to meet people to ask out, and second, it's where I learned the rules of the dating game. A group of us would sit around talking after an activity or event, and often the topic would be dating. I heard girls talk about good and bad dating experiences, well-seasoned daters talk about things they have discovered, and the socially challenged talk about their own struggles. Actually, the latter were often the most insightful, partly because others offered them great advice and partly because I was among the socially challenged ones asking questions!

I've already mentioned that my top activity recommendation is institute. I could go on for the rest of the book about why this is such a great venue, but instead, I'll just touch briefly on why I appreciate it so much.

How I Met Jenni

As my first semester of institute came to a close, the institute announced that it would be providing a summer class called, "Crossing the Plains." It was a whole institute class dedicated entirely to the Mormon pioneer trek west. In that class, we would discuss all that happened along that trail, and then as soon as the semester ended, there would be a four-day pioneer trek where we'd ride up to Wyoming and see all the major pioneer sites from Wyoming to Salt Lake. The trip was well planned and organized.

There had been two "Crossing the Plains" classes, one in the day, and one at night. The night class was the largest, which I attended. The trek was a combination of both classes. Many of the day class members included some of the new West and Granite High school graduates, this being their first institute class. The first time I met the morning class group was on the morning of the trek.

Among that group was a young, sweet, and beautiful girl named Jenni Hair. I was introduced to her that morning, and though she certainly caught my eye, she was a little bit young. Only a couple months earlier I had been turned down for a second date with a girl who was only a few months younger than Jenni. The girl had turned me down because her parents didn't like the age difference. That had been a little embarrassing. I wasn't ready to make that mistake again, so I didn't ask Jenni out. But Jenni and I did become friends during the trek.

The funny thing about age difference is that if you're willing to wait, the gap will shrink. Four years younger is a little too much for a fresh returned missionary, but for a twenty-four-year old, it's totally fine. So after knowing each other about a year and a half, we were close enough in age that I decided to ask her out. That was a very active time in my dating life, and though we actually dated on or off a couple times, by the time nine months had past, we decided to be exclusive and only date each other. I won't go into detail about the bumpy ride that finally got us to that point, but I can say that I learned a lot about both myself and my feelings for Jenni during that time.

Many of our experiences together were a "first." Jenni was the first girl I ever held hands with or kissed, and I was her first as well. We fell in love, and before long, we just couldn't seem to get enough of each other.

Our growing relationship was a perfect example of how a person can fail and fail and fail, and then out of nowhere, suddenly experience success. Every married couple I talk to about the circumstances of their meeting has a similar story. It almost feels like pure luck that things work out, but nothing happens by chance when we put the Lord first in our lives.

thirty

~

Creating a Universe

I don't think I was fully aware of it at the time, but Jenni and I were creating a small universe for ourselves. Creating a universe with someone takes time and effort, but when it's with someone you really care about, it's really quite easy. Soon we were so wrapped up in each other that I'm sure our siblings and friends felt out of place in our presence. But now I realize that this was not a bad thing. In fact, it's probably a necessary part of building life with someone.

Just like building anything, when you want to build a life with someone, you have to start small. During those early stages that precede and sometimes carry on into engagement, a couple becomes so involved in this new and growing universe that they can easily become oblivious to the happenings around them. Though they try hard to be attentive to other responsibilities, I've never been one to condemn this exclusiveness. It's an important part of creating a lasting relationship. These oblivious realms can act as a seed to the deep and open communication that is necessary in a healthy marriage.

After marriage, these "exclusive" talks may not be as obvious to outsiders, because the couple can have these private moments much more easily and much more often.

Deciding that I wanted to marry Jenni was not a difficult choice to make. I knew that's what I wanted. But I wanted to make sure the

Lord was okay with it. So I went to the temple one afternoon, and after doing an ordinance, I went and spent some time in the celestial room.

I've found it easier to get answers to prayers while in the temple than any other place. Answers rarely come without effort, but God always answers prayers. But God also often leaves choices in our hands, and this was one of those times. I didn't get a clear answer, though I had felt the Lord's permission to date Jenni many times.

It's interesting to note the times in our lives when the Lord gives clear and specific answers and when He leaves choices up to us. For me, not receiving a clear answer to this prayer, in which I was making the most important decision of my life, was an indication of the Lord's incredible faith in me to make the right decision. It also meant that I would be the one to choose my eternal companion. Though it would have been nice to receive a clear answer, I was actually grateful that the Lord left the final decision to me.

I had paid the price in preparation, fasting, prayer, and worthiness to receive an answer from the Lord. While my heart was full of peace, the answer didn't come. In that state of mind, I told the Lord that I planned on asking Jenni to marry me, and I requested that if He did not approve of this action that He might make it clear to me.

Again, no clear direction came, so I went forward with my decision. I'm so grateful that I didn't sit at home and wait for the answer. I went forward in confidence. I was confident that I was making a wise decision and that the Lord confirmed it but felt He was allowing me to make my own choice. I suppose if I'd had doubts and inhibitions, I might have held off. But I was sure that Jenni was the one I wanted to spend my life—and eternity—with and from what I could tell, the Lord approved of my decision. Some people make the mistake of thinking if things come up in their lives, such as a series of unfortunate circumstances—the car breaks down, you lose a job, your phone breaks—that the Lord is trying to send the message that your decision isn't right. But I don't know of a circumstance where the Lord has tried to physically step in the way of a prayerful decision except in a few cases when a person is *not* coming to Him for answers. Usually He answers through feelings, impressions, scriptures, and the words of His living servants. Don't think if you lose a contact lens that the Lord is telling you not to marry your boyfriend. He may allow things to happen that test your character and build patience to prepare you for big decisions, but if you're striving to receive answers in prayer, He will tell you directly in His own time and way.

A few days after my visit to the temple, I went to meet Jenni at her work. She still had about an hour left, so I pulled out my homework. Then I remembered that Sugarhouse Park was right across the street, so I told Jenni I would go do my homework there and be back before she got off.

It was a beautiful spring evening, and as I studied, it occurred to me that this park would be an ideal place to propose to Jenni. Not only was it a peaceful, beautiful location, but it was where we'd had our first date.

That evening I planned my scheme. A couple days later we were scheduled to have another date—an afternoon date to Donut Falls. If I could convince her afterwards to stop by Sugarhouse Park for a bit . . .

The day before the date, I went to The Flower Patch and ordered eleven roses of varying colors (but none that were a deep red), and clipped a note to each that said, "I love you because . . ." and then listed some reason I loved Jenni. I even numbered them from twelve to two, making it obvious that number one was missing. I placed the order so they would be delivered to her before she left for work and before our date.

Then I purchased a single deep red rose with all the decoration of a full bouquet and attached a longer note telling her how much I loved her. I told her that the number one reason I loved her was because she loved the Lord more than she loved me. I don't know how romantic that statement is, but it meant a great deal to me. I knew that if both of us put the Lord first in our lives, our marriage would work beautifully.

Then I took the decked out red rose with the note and hid it in some bushes at Sugarhouse Park. Then I headed home for the night, knowing that things were in motion. Tomorrow I would ask Jenni to marry me.

The morning was beautiful, and I could tell from the start that I'd chosen the right day to propose. The sun was out, and it was warm, but there was a cool breeze, so the climate was perfect.

After Jenni got off work, we drove to Donut Falls. On the way, she thanked me for the flowers and talked about how much fun it was to read each little message. Then she said, "But where's number one?" I'd had plans to act surprised and complain that they must have messed up my order—but I chickened out and said, "You'll see." I'm sure this roused her curiosity, but it renewed the tension in my nerves.

While at the falls, I realized that this might be a better location to propose, but it was too late—my plan was already underway.

Hand in hand, we went back down the trail. We walked everywhere hand in hand by this time.

Jenni had a short meeting to attend at her ward house, so we drove to her meeting. I waited patiently in the halls of the church, knowing the time was short. Did she have any clue what I was up to? Was she ready to have me propose? Would she panic? Would she need more time? I knew she loved me—she'd told me many times. But was she ready for marriage?

I tried to keep my knees from rattling as she got out of her meeting. What if my voice cracked? What if she didn't fall for my plan?

We got back in her car. "Hey, while you were in there, I remembered something," I said, trying to act casual—as if I wasn't on the verge of an anxiety attack. "Remember how I went and did homework at Sugarhouse park the other day while you were at work?"

"Yes."

"Well, I think I may have dropped some of my notes while I was studying." Instantly I thought my reasoning sounded ridiculous, but there was no turning back now. "Normally I wouldn't care, but I have a test coming up, and they're the notes from the review. Would it be okay if we stop and just look around to see if they're still there?

I mean, they're probably gone by now, but it's worth a try . . ." I felt silly, but she didn't seem to sense it.

We drove to Sugarhouse Park, and I lead her to the area where I'd been "doing homework."

"I was right next to the river . . ." I told her. "I'm sure it was near here. How about you check there, and I'll check up stream a bit."

She agreed, and I headed for the bushes where I'd hid the flower. Thank heaven, it was still there and it hadn't rained. What a nightmare that would have been! Saying a quick prayer, I turned and walked back toward Jenni.

When she saw me coming with a large rose, decked out like a bouquet, her face turned into a playful, "So *that's* what this is all about" look.

"You wondered about number one—this is it." Then I handed her the flower with the note, and she read it while I stood by waiting. When she looked up, I told her that I loved her, and that I could think of no one I'd rather spend eternity with. "I want to invite you to be my eternal companion," I said, now feeling more excitement than anxiety. Then, getting on my knees, I asked, "Jenni, will you marry me?"

Despite being a little overwhelmed, she managed a yes. We hugged and kissed a bit and then started heading back to the car, both of us barely aware of the world around us. Neither of us could believe that we were actually engaged. As we headed back to the car, Jenni said that in her excitement, she couldn't remember whether she had said, "Yes" when I asked. I assured her that she had. "Oh, good!" she replied.

We went to the Old Spaghetti Factory for dinner, which was Jenni's favorite restaurant, all the while talking about our plans and hopes for the future.

After coming home in the evening, it felt strange to think that I was actually getting married. *I* was getting married—and to the most incredible, beautiful, and amazing girl in the whole world.

The next few weeks went by in a whirl of activity. There was so much to do and very little time. We decided to get married about three months after getting engaged. We soon discovered that this was an almost ideal amount of time for us. We had a lot to do. There were invitations to make, a dress and tux to order, cake, flowers, bouquets, and decorations to order, reservations to make, a honeymoon to plan, and a temple to call. Not to mention the ordinary day-to-day things that already kept us quite busy. Other than an official weekly date, there was very little time to spare.

Some would say that three months is too short to properly plan a wedding, but that's only one side of the issue. For us, once we were engaged, we no longer carried any doubts about each other's feelings and having made lifetime—and even eternal commitments—to each other, the bond and attraction we had for each other increased. It was difficult to be apart, and the more we were together, the stronger the physical temptation was. Our communication was even more personal and more meaningful than before.

For us, waiting an unnecessary amount of time to make the covenant we had already committed to make would have been both unwise and ridiculous. It was the ordinance that mattered, not the detailed wedding arrangements. We wanted to be sealed to each other, and all the decorations and reservations meant nothing compared with that. Besides, an engagement is not intended to be a long-term commitment. The longer a couple waits, the more likely they are to either get into trouble or get cold feet—and both problems go completely away after the marriage takes place. Many couples wait too long and find that the delay was a big mistake—or at best, totally unnecessary.

Another mistake many engaged couples make is that they spend so much energy planning the wedding that they forget to plan the marriage. They have a beautiful wedding day, but after the honeymoon, they discover that they don't know each other nearly as well as they thought.

Jenni and I were aware of this potential problem, and we worked hard to prevent it by talking a *lot*. We made special effort to talk about what kind of life we wanted to have together and about financial and academic goals and how to fulfill them. We talked about how many kids we wanted and discussed child-raising strategies. In doing so, we realized how serious a matter marriage is, and it made us that much more eager to get married and covenant ourselves entirely to each other.

When you get married, you are truly giving yourself to your partner—and not just figuratively. You are making covenants to put your spouse's needs above your own. There are many big choices you'll make in life, such as what to study in school, what kind of career you will pursue, or where you will buy a home. Those decisions can be made with the idea, "I'll try this out for a while, but if it doesn't work out for me, I'll move on to something else."

Marriage is not such a decision. There is a massive amount of faith in this choice, and there is no question, no second guessing, and no backing out once that covenant is made. You have made your choice. Now honor, protect, and perfect that choice.

Jeffrey R. Holland said:

> No serious courtship or engagement or marriage is worth the name if we do not fully invest all that we have in it and in so doing trust ourselves totally to the one we love. You cannot succeed in love if you keep one foot out on the bank for safety's sake. The very nature of the endeavor requires that you hold on to each other as tightly as you can and jump in the pool together. In that spirit, and in the spirit of Mormon's plea for pure love, I want to impress upon you the vulnerability and delicacy of your partner's future as it is placed in your hands for safekeeping—male and female, it works both ways.[1]

Certainly, by the time you are approaching marriage, you have thought a great deal about the risks you are taking in marrying this girl. Have you ever stopped to consider what a terribly horrid risk your wife-to-be is making? For heaven's sake! She is marrying *you*! You would do well to make every effort *not* to disappoint her. After all, she has also made eternal covenants, and promised her heart, soul, and body to you. That's not something to be taken lightly. More than any other person on earth, you have tremendous power to bring her joy, but you also have more power than anyone on earth to bring her pain and heartache. You will come to know her more intimately and personally than any other person on earth. You would do well to consider Elder Holland's counsel:

> The result is that I know much more clearly now how to help her, and, if I let myself, I know exactly what will hurt her. In the honesty of our love—love that can't truly be Christlike without such total devotion—surely God will hold me accountable for any pain I cause her by intentionally exploiting or hurting her when she has been so trusting of me, having long since thrown away any self-protection in order that we could be, as the scripture says, "one flesh" (Genesis 2:24). To impair or impede her in any way for my gain or vanity or emotional mastery over her should disqualify me on the spot to be her husband. Indeed, it should consign my miserable soul to eternal incarceration in that large and spacious building Lehi says is the prison of those who live by "vain imaginations" and the "pride of the world" (1 Nephi 11:36, 12:18). No wonder that building is at the opposite end of the field from the tree of life representing the love of God! In all that Christ was, He was not ever envious or inflated, never consumed with His own needs. He did not once, not ever, seek His own advantage at the expense of someone else. He delighted in the happiness of others, the happiness He could bring them. He was forever kind.[2]

In the same fireside, Sister Patricia Holland said:

> Every mortal marriage is to recreate the ideal marriage sought by Adam and Eve, by Jehovah and the children of Israel. With no hanging back, "cleaving unto none other," each fragile human spirit is left naked, as it were, in the custody of its marriage partner, even as our first parents were in that beautiful garden setting. Surely that is a risk. Certainly it is an act of faith. But the risk is central to the meaning of the marriage and the faith moves mountains and calms the turbulent sea."[3]

Marriage is truly awesome. It requires a level of spiritual, physical, and emotional maturity that is almost more than can be reasonably expected of any of us, but which maturity is part of our innermost divine nature. That is why we must step into marriage entirely, without holding back—God has ordained that marriage should be eternal, and it acts as a catalyst to our divine potential. If we approach it with humility, eternal love, and pure worthiness, then marriage can make gods of us, in every sense of the word. That doesn't mean marriage makes righteousness easier, but it does mean that if we are willing to approach marriage the way God intends, then it can make us into the people God intends us to be.

NOTES

1. Holland, "How Do I Love Thee?"
2. Ibid.
3. Holland, "Some Things We Have Learned—Together."

thirty-one

~

Why Not Today?

During one of our regular talks together, I mentioned to Jenni that I hoped that we could start early to read scriptures together as a family.

"In fact," I said as the discussion progressed, "why don't we commit ourselves to begin the day after our wedding day, so we can know that we started our marriage with that as a tradition."

Then Jenni taught me a great lesson about both her own dedication and about starting righteous traditions when she replied, "But we don't really have to wait till we're married. Why don't we start today?"

Again I was impressed by this amazing woman.

So we started that day. Every day that we were together, we made sure to include reading scriptures.

That experience renewed in my heart the lesson that it rarely works to make a resolution that you don't intend to start keeping immediately. Why wait till New Year's or your birthday, or even tomorrow if there is any way to begin immediately? You have the determination right now—you are ready to run with it right now. If you wait, that fire may dwindle before you even get started. Just the effort made in that first attempt may give you the momentum to help you keep your resolution even after the fire is gone.

Another thing about resolutions. Many people give up on a resolution after a few failed attempts. They may feel that they just don't have the personality or stamina for it. But the only thing that stands between you and your goal is your choices. You must choose to start, and you must choose to follow through. You can make a decision once and simply stick to it, telling yourself that you've already made the choice to do the thing, and you no longer have the right to choose otherwise.

Is that a forfeiture of agency? No, that is the very essence of agency. You made the choice, and you followed through. One who hasn't the strength to keep a resolution has simply forfeited their agency to the whims of the moment. He will never have real agency until he lets nothing stand between him and his decision.

thirty-two

Revolutionizing the Course of the Universe

It was a very dull day at Deseret Book as I leaned on the counter, chin in hands, waiting for something to happen. One of my coworkers stood only a few feet away, as bored as I was.

"So," I said, trying to break the monotony, "what should I do to revolutionize the course of the world today?"

He thought a moment. "Got any bombs? You could always blow up an important building somewhere."

"That's true. But I don't have any bombs. Besides, that's a bad thing, and there are plenty of bad things going on all the time. I need to find something good to do."

"That's true," he replied. Then we both fell back into silence.

I began thinking more about our silly conversation. What could one do to revolutionize the course of the world? What about the universe? Could one person really affect the destiny of the universe? Is that possible?

Many people have changed the course of life on this planet. Thomas Edison invented the light bulb. George Washington led a revolutionary war that led to the foundation of what might be considered the most powerful nation in world history. But did those things change the destiny of the universe?

It occurred to me that the person who best altered the course of the universe would have to be Jesus Christ. Not only did He alter the destiny of every person in the universe, but He provided a way for us to become like His Father.

That thought brought on a new approach to the question. If I have potential to become like my Father in Heaven, then certainly I have power to affect the destiny of the universe. If we live worthy to obtain eternal life, we will continue to have eternal children for all time. Now that's revolutionary!

So I guess the next question would be, what can I do today to best affect that progress? Of course, a response as broad as "live the gospel" wasn't really sufficient, since I had been striving to do that my whole life.

Then I realized that I was in the process of beginning one of the major aspects of the perfecting process. I was about to get married in the temple to a worthy young woman. I decided that maybe the best thing I can do to work toward that goal is to strengthen my relationship with Jenni. How can I do that? That question is easy. I can be kind and loving to her.

I looked around the store. Everything was quiet, normal, ordinary. Customers came in, looked around, and left. Employees straightened bookshelves or stood patiently, waiting for something to happen.

I had a date with Jenni scheduled for that night. I decided that tonight I would change the course of the universe—I would show more love and kindness toward her.

After Marriage

And again, verily I say unto you, if a man marry a wife by my word, which is my law, and by the new and everlasting covenant, and it is sealed unto them by the Holy Spirit of promise, by him who is anointed, unto whom I have appointed this power and the keys of this priesthood; . . . it shall be done unto them in all things whatsoever my servant hath put upon them, in time, and through all eternity; and shall be of full force when they are out of the world; and they shall pass by the angels, and the gods, which are set there, to their exaltation and glory in all things, as hath been sealed upon their heads, which glory shall be a fulness and a continuation of the seeds forever and ever.
—D&C 132:19

thirty-three

~~~~~~

Get Ready,
Get Set . . . Marry!

Was I ready to get married? Of course not. Was Jenni ready? No. How can anyone be ready to make an eternal commitment with the severely limited mortal understanding that this life confines us to? Is anyone really ready for marriage? I don't think so. The point is not to be ready. The point is to be worthy and willing to trust in the Lord and His ability to direct our feeble minds in a decision we are not even close to ready to make.

Marriage, more than just about any other decision, is an act of faith. Faith in God, faith in our spouse-to-be, and most challenging, faith in ourselves. Of course, there are necessary preparations, especially as they deal with emotional and spiritual maturity. But emotional and spiritual maturity are primarily matters of worthiness and humility. The Lord can help us develop those during every stage of life, and though it will take decades to develop the maturity that makes us fully prepared for marriage, it wouldn't work to wait until then to marry.

Did I marry the perfect wife for me? Yes. Is she perfect? No. Am I perfect? Of course not. Were we ready to get married? No. But that's what mortality is about—taking righteous steps into the unknown and allowing the Lord to carry us along as we develop the attributes necessary to make it work.

Ready or not, the day came. Our sealing was to take place at 10:30 a.m., but we wanted to attend an endowment session beforehand. That turned out to be a great way to prepare for the ceremony. As with all wedding days, ours started out early and busy. We had decided to marry in the Mount Timpanogos Temple, so in order to make the 8:00 a.m. session, we had to leave by about 6:00, and with travel time and all the preparations we had to make, we had to get up at 4:00 a.m.

We had found an apartment in Salt Lake, and for the last few weeks before the wedding, I lived in the apartment. I got ready as fast as I could and headed over to Jenni's house. Any opportunity to keep the tradition of the groom not seeing the bride before the wedding was smashed by 4:30 a.m.

After the rush and hustle, we made it in good time for the session. Everyone was so kind to us. They went out of their way to congratulate us and make it a special experience for us.

It was indeed a special experience. At the beginning of the session, I was nervous and a little anxious. I wasn't having cold feet, but I knew what I was about to do, and the idea was a little intimidating. But the Spirit was strong in the session, and by its end, all my anxieties had changed to love, peace, and almost overwhelming joy. As the celestial room slowly cleared out, we got to spend a few minutes alone together. What a great opportunity as we prepared to become eternal companions! We knew it wouldn't be long before family started arriving, but for a few minutes it was just me, Jenni, and the Lord.

Our sealer was Elder Jack H. Goaslind. He had been our institute teacher for a time, and as an emeritus member of the Seventy, he could do sealings in any temple worldwide.

I could describe all the details of that day—with the fabulous wedding brunch, the almost overwhelming reception, and the tired feet and limbs—but those things hardly compare to the constant feeling of love and gratitude I felt for and from Jenni and everyone who came to congratulate and celebrate with us.

The feelings were especially strong as we stood in the reception line greeting the visitors. I had dreaded the line, but seeing so many old and new friends and family was so uplifting that I hardly noticed my numb feet. People kept coming, so by the time the line ended, we had to hurry and cut the cake so we could leave for our honeymoon before it got too late. After throwing the bouquet, bidding everyone farewell, and a quick change of clothes at Jenni's house, we sped off in my dad's tastefully decorated truck—signs and balloons waving in the wind.

thirty-four

~~~

The Honeymoon

I won't say much about our honeymoon except that it was a wonderful experience. I will mention a couple things that we had learned prior to our honeymoon that might help another couple with their own.

What happens on a honeymoon is between you and your new spouse. People will ask you where you went on your honeymoon, but they won't ask details about what you did. It's an interesting transition, going from single to married—all in a day. Before the wedding, there were so many necessary guardrails and standards. Those guardrails have to be strong and consistent. After the wedding, all the actions that were so forbidden before marriage suddenly became totally acceptable and even expected.

This does not mean, however, that the couple must leap out of their comfort zones and do more than they feel ready to do. The secret is good, appropriate, open communication.

If a couple talks about what they expect on their wedding night prior to the marriage, they will feel much better about it when the time comes. Since this is brand-new territory for both, don't worry about taking it slow. Turning off all the lights and going to bed in pajamas may even help the couple feel more comfortable going to bed together. After all, they have the rest of their lives to develop romantic skills. The husband and wife are the only two people who will ever know exactly what happened on the honeymoon. Just do what is comfortable for both of you, and you'll find that your body knows its job and will guide you along.

Some fear that if they date someone who wishes to abstain from physical intimacy (or even just passionate kissing or making out) before marriage that they will want to abstain *after* marriage—or perhaps abstain until it's time to have kids. In my observation, this is simply not true. Most people know that after marriage, sex is good, right, and can be shared as often as the couple desires, and in whatever manner is enjoyable for both. Again, the secret is open communication during engagement.

You should probably talk as a couple and decide on some basic guidelines for yourselves ahead of time so that neither of you will feel hurt or frightened after marriage. You should also both be willing to talk as you go along. The movies know nothing about communication, and you are stepping into undiscovered territory.

Be patient with each other, try most of all to please your partner, and have a sense of humor. Humor keeps the mood light and makes communication much easier.

Remember it's *your* honeymoon. Focus on each other, and just have a great time together. You'll be surprised at how fast you become a pro at romance if you just take it easy and enjoy each other. Sex is a beautiful and sacred thing.

Jeffrey R. Holland advised:

> I wish to stress, as my third of three reasons to be clean, that sexual union is also, in its own profound way, a very real sacrament of the highest order, a union not only of a man and a woman but also very much the union of that man and woman with God. Indeed, if our definition of sacrament is that act of claiming and sharing and exercising God's own inestimable power, then I know of virtually no other divine privilege so routinely given to us all—women or men, ordained or unordained, Latter-day Saint or non-Latter-day Saint—than the miraculous and majestic power of transmitting life, the unspeakable, unfathomable, unbroken power of procreation. There are those special moments in our lives when the other, more

formal ordinances of the gospel—the sacraments, if you will—allow us to feel the grace and grandeur of God's power. Many are one-time experiences (such as our own confirmation or our own marriage), and some are repeatable (such as administering to the sick or doing ordinance work for others in the temple). But I know of nothing so earth-shatteringly powerful and yet so universally and unstintingly given to us as the God-given power available in every one of us from our early teen years on to create a human body, that wonder of all wonders, a genetically and spiritually unique being never seen before in the history of the world and never to be duplicated again in all the ages of eternity—a child, your child—with eyes and ears and fingers and toes and a future of unspeakable grandeur.[1]

Some suggest that the *only* purpose for sex is to have children. This is simply not true. While that may be its most obvious purpose, sex is also intended for strengthening the marriage relationship. It can strengthen bonds, relieve stress, and encourage other types of emotional intimacy. The key is unselfishness. Sex never was an evil, selfish, or dirty thing, though the devil has worked hard to turn it into that. It is a beautiful and righteous thing, so sacred that it can only appropriately take place in marriage.

Your honeymoon may be an introduction to that aspect of marriage, but when and how you go about it is entirely up to the two of you.

NOTE

1. Holland, "Of Souls, Symbols, and Sacraments," 78–79.

thirty-five

The First Year

Despite many people's warning that things would get tough after the honeymoon, we found that married life was fantastic. You might say the honeymoon continued, even with work, school, and financial stress.

We were able to rent an apartment in South Salt Lake, which was close to where Jenni grew up, and close to work and school.

During our first two months of marriage, we had no car. Some would say this is impractical, but to us, it was just life. We had been determined to get married, whatever our circumstances, and we've never regretted it.

We did find one advantage to not having a car. Jenni worked about a mile from home, and I went to school about a mile and a half from home in the same direction. We chose to walk to work and school in the morning, and then take the bus home at night. Those morning walks were one of the greatest helps during those early weeks of our marriage. The key to adjusting to marriage, with all its ramifications, is communication, and these morning walks provided that opportunity.

We had a lot of fun on these walks too. Sometimes we would play a game where we would watch the people in the cars that drove by to see if the driver looks like their vehicle. Some did too!

Sometimes we would make up stories about the drivers.

"This next one is Mr. Phil Wooper." I would tell Jenni. "He's headed to his job at the duck farm, where he herds ducks—all day. Oh, and here comes Bertha Boondoggle. She's the founder of *Jerky Works*, which makes the best jerky east of the Jordon and west of State Street."

Then Jenni would continue, "Yes, but she's actually been working the graveyard shift, and now she's headed to 7-Eleven to get a hot dog for breakfast."

We also found it entertaining to kick stuff we found on our way, such as plastic bottles, fallen apples, and rocks. One day we even came across a semi-flat rubber ball—you know the ones that come in the huge baskets at the grocery store. It was sitting in the gutter, and for us, it was better than any rock or plastic bottle. So we kicked it down the street.

We had kicked the ball about a quarter mile, having much success keeping it from rolling out of range, when I got up the courage to give it a full-power running kick. The ball shot out and forward and then took an extreme turn toward the house ahead of us.

The flying ball slammed into the front door of the house with a loud *BANG*. We cowered, looking for a tree to hide behind in case the people inside came to see what had hit their door. It was early in the morning, so a sound like that would wake a light sleeper. So you can imagine our feelings when a middle-aged woman—looking terribly shaken—stood up from a chair sitting next to the door.

She had been just out of sight. When she stood up and stepped into view, we were so shocked to see her, and she was so shocked to see that it was a young couple walking by rather than some rowdy teenagers, that all we could say was, "Sorry!"

We picked up our ball from the lawn and walked on. When we were out of sight, we laughed uncontrollably.

Only a block or two further, we were still kicking our ball. Jenni gave it a good kick. Then, out of nowhere, a massive German Shepherd bolted after it, grabbed it, and ran off with it. Now we were laughing so hard we had to sit down to catch our breath.

Laughter, love, and patience carried us through those first few months, and though it was a big adjustment, we both far preferred married life to single life. We loved being together and got into a habit of doing everything together. That habit helped us set a pattern of family priority.

thirty-six

~~~

Adjusting Together

As tight as things were financially, we found that the secret to financial security is tithing. We determined from the very start to always, *always,* pay an honest full tithe. That made up the difference. I've heard some say that when you use tithing math, it all adds up, even if regular math doesn't. We found that to be remarkably true. When you pay tithing, things work out.

We were also blessed to start marriage without any debt. We decided never to get any consumer debt. We knew that we would maybe need to take out loans for education or required payments for doctor bills—not to mention a huge loan for purchasing a home—but we were determined to never get into unnecessary consumer debt.

President J. Reuben Clark said:

> It is a rule of our financial and economic life in all the world that interest is to be paid on borrowed money. May I say something about interest?
>
> Interest never sleeps nor sickens nor dies; it never goes to the hospital; it works on Sundays and holidays; it never takes a vacation; . . . it is never laid off work . . . it buys no food; it wears no clothes; it is unhoused; . . . it has neither weddings nor births nor deaths; it has no love, no sympathy; it is as hard and soulless as a granite cliff. Once in debt, [it] is your companion every minute of the day and night; you cannot shun it or slip away from it; you cannot

dismiss it; . . . and whenever you get in its way or cross its course or fail to meet its demands, it crushes you.[1]

Finances comprises one of those areas that can cause great contention if there isn't communication, understanding, and self-discipline. Keep in mind that no matter what you don't have, you *do* have each other. Remember that by the time you were engaged, no material thing was worth anything if it kept the two of you apart. You wouldn't have cared if you'd have had to live the rest of your life in a broken barn if it meant you could be together. Who cares if you don't have all the things that your parents took decades to accumulate? *You have each other!*

Gordon B. Hinckley advised:

> Be modest in your wants. You do not need a big home with a big mortgage as you begin your lives together. You can and should avoid overwhelming debt. There is nothing that will cause greater tensions in marriage than grinding debt, which will make of you a slave to your creditors. You may have to borrow money to begin ownership of a home. But do not let it be so costly that it will preoccupy your thoughts day and night.
>
> When I was married my wise father said to me, "Get a modest home and pay off the mortgage so that if economic storms should come, your wife and children will have a roof over their heads." . . .
>
> Unless there is full and complete understanding between you and your wife on these matters, there likely will come misunderstandings and suspicions that will cause trouble that can lead to greater problems.[2]

The Lord always provides a way when we strive to follow his commandments.

Jenni and I discovered things about each other that were impossible to know before we were married. While these discoveries could have led to contention, they usually led to understanding and sometimes humor.

Two people coming from two totally different backgrounds will make an amusing match no matter how much they had in common before they were married.

One thing that helped us work through these differences was

to laugh at them—not at each other but at the irony that we would see the same things so differently. We even started keeping a family journal, which included a page of Hathawayisms and Hairisms.

This led to many amusing discussions, including a time we had to call both sets of parents to see which of our families called the little white things you put in the dryer *fabric softener*, and who called them *dryer sheets*. As it turned out, they are two different things . . .

I once heard it said that a couple should use their similarities to understand each other, and their differences to complement each other. This is good advice. Your spouse's hurried nature may seem to clash with your tendency to be laid back, but having that difference will help you each develop some of the attribute you lack. Where one spouse is weak, the other may be strong, and each can offer support and help. Where both are weak or strong, they can understand and lean on each other, working together for a common goal. Differences never need to become catastrophes. They can be learning experiences. Remember that if your spouse feels vulnerable, that is when patience and understanding will mean the most to them.

Our differences occasionally led to negative reactions, such as mild arguments. We never shouted at each other, but sometimes a disagreement led to hurt feelings. These were always painful, but I think even in these instances, we discovered our personal weaknesses—some of which we didn't know we had before marriage, but by working through these differences, we grew to understand each other better.

Actually, I quickly came to discover that marriage is not hard at all. Marriage is wonderful, rewarding, supportive, and exciting. Life, however, is hard. Life is terribly difficult and is absolutely full of challenges—more than one person can handle alone.

When we experience life's challenges and then blame the marriage, or we take out our frustrations with life on our spouse, we have major problems.

Why is it that we let the problems of life ruin the relationship that has the greatest power to get us through it? If we remember that life is hard, and marriage is wonderful, then it will be easy to maintain proper perspective when times get tough.

Jeffrey R. Holland counseled:

> As a youth in England, Samuel Plimsoll was fascinated with watching ships load and unload their cargoes. He soon observed that, regardless of the cargo space available, each ship had its maximum capacity. If a ship exceeded its limit, it would likely sink at sea. In 1868 Plimsoll entered Parliament and passed a merchant shipping act that, among other things, called for making calculations of how much a ship could carry. As a result, lines were drawn on the hull of each ship in England. As the cargo was loaded, the freighter would sink lower and lower into the water. When the water level on the side of the ship reached the Plimsoll mark, the ship was considered loaded to capacity, regardless of how much space remained. As a result, British deaths at sea were greatly reduced.
>
> Like ships, people have differing capacities at different times and even different days in their lives. In our relationships we need to establish our own Plimsoll marks and help identify them in the lives of those we love. Together we need to monitor the load levels and be helpful in shedding or at least readjusting some cargo if we see our sweetheart is sinking. Then, when the ship of love is stabilized, we can evaluate long-term what has to continue, what can be put off until another time, and what can be put off permanently. Friends, sweethearts, and spouses need to be able to monitor each other's stress and recognize the different tides and seasons of life.[3]

While dating often requires alternating between the choice to love and the choice to not love the person you are dating, after marriage you must *always* choose to love your spouse. You must also always choose *not* to take interest in all others of the opposite sex.

That choice to love your spouse must be made every day. You must make the initial covenant that you will always choose to love your spouse, and then you must renew that promise every single day.

While showing and demonstrating love is easy while you are dating or engaged, and even early in a marriage, distractions that will make it easy to forget to do those simple acts of love that keep a marriage alive. Be patient with your companion, and be patient with yourself.

Jeffrey R. Holland said:

> It would be worth our time with you today if we could impress
> upon you the sacred obligation a husband and wife have to each
> other when the fragility and vulnerability and delicacy of the part-
> ner's life is placed in the other's keeping. Pat and I have lived together
> for twenty-two years, as she said earlier—roughly the time that each
> of us had lived alone prior to the wedding day. I may not know every-
> thing about her, but I know twenty-two years' worth, and she knows
> that much of me. I know her likes and dislikes, and she knows mine.
> I know her tastes and interests and hopes and dreams, and she knows
> mine. As our love has grown and our relationship matured, we have
> been increasingly open with each other about all of that for twenty-
> two years now, and the result is that I know much more clearly how
> to help her and I know exactly how to hurt her. I may not know
> all the buttons to push, but I know most of them. And surely God
> will hold me accountable for any pain I cause her by intentionally
> pushing the hurtful ones when she has been so trusting of me. To
> toy with such a sacred trust—her body, her spirit, and her eternal
> future—and exploit those for my gain, even if only emotional gain,
> should disqualify me to be her husband and ought to consign my
> miserable soul to hell.[4]

It also helps to remember that while your spouse is your eternal
companion, they are also God's child. He knows your spouse better
than you do. If you stay close to the Lord, He will enlighten and
inspire you to know how to reach out to and bless your companion.

One thing that can help in trying to show love for your spouse
is to get to know what it takes for your spouse to feel loved. The
two of you may have a great deal in common, but remember you're
still from different backgrounds. You both have different ways of
expressing and receiving love. If you haven't read it already, I highly
recommend that you get the book *The Five Love Languages* by Gary
Chapman. In it, he explains that while one spouse may feel most
loved when their spouse does the dishes for them, the other might
feel most loved when they are being hugged.

Specifically, Dr. Chapman identifies five areas of expressing and
receiving love. He suggests that in some form or another, everyone is
a native speaker in one of these areas: physical touch, receiving gifts,

words of affirmation, quality time, and acts of service. Obviously every person is different, and the *type* of touch, gift, words, time, or service will change with each individual, but learning your spouse's primary love language will empower you to show the most love to them in the way they will want to receive it. Not only may it save you both a lot of heartache, but it will save a lot of time. She may be working long hours to make sure the dishes and laundry are spotless before bedtime to show her husband how much she loves him when it would mean so much more to him if she would just sit and talk to him for a few minutes each day.

Don't assume that what you want from your spouse is exactly what your spouse wants from you. Find out what your spouse wants, and give it to them.

NOTES

1. J. Reuben Clark, Jr., Conference Report, Apr. 1938, 103.
2. Hinckley, "Living Worthy of the Girl You Will Someday Marry," 49.
3. Holland, "How Do I Love Thee?"
4. Holland, "Some Things We Have Learned—Together."

Conclusion:

The Adventure Begins

What else is there to say about my first year of marriage? Jenni and I loved each other, and we were excited to spend eternity together. Although our journey was just barely beginning, we would be taking the journey together.

I felt like I'd completed an important mission—the mission to find my eternal companion. Jenni is mine forever. Obviously we have to live worthy of the fulfillment of that promise, but nothing and no one can take that from us outside of our own agency. She is mine, and I am hers.

Not long before the end of that first year, I learned that I was starting another mission. I had already served a full-time mission for two years, and then it had taken me about four years to find Jenni. So far every new life mission had been more interesting, more frightening, and more rewarding than the last. I knew this new mission would be no exception. Some returned missionaries say that the mission field was the best two years of their life. For me, the first two years of marriage were the best two years—so far.

Were we ready for our next mission? No. Who is ever ready for a whole new phase of life? But we were living right, and though neither of us could take on this new mission alone, we would do it together. I think missions come in the order they do because we gain something from the last mission that will be necessary for the coming mission. We were a team, and we would take on our new mission as a team.

Our adventure together had only just begun. What was our new mission? Nine months after we got married, we learned that Jenni was pregnant.

Marriage really is awesome. When Jenni and I were about to marry, people would see us so happy together. As if we were headed for doom, they would say, "Well, just wait till you're married. The first year is the hardest. Life will hit you in the face, you'll see each other's quirks, and you'll see what marriage is *really* like." Okay, so they didn't say it that ominously, but people would warn us it was going to get harder, and although some things do get harder, I have my own thoughts about what that means.

By the time I'd been married nine months, I felt great. I loved Jenni, I loved being married to her, and I wondered what people meant when they said the first year is the worst. In fact, I remember thinking, "Man, if this is the hardest, I've got it made!"

We knew life would get tougher. We knew it would get tighter, scarier, busier, and more hectic. Our greatest challenges were in the future, but we also knew it would get more exciting, more fun, and more rewarding. We would take it one day at a time—sometimes one moment at a time. We also knew that we weren't just products of society. We had been sealed in the temple. We had agency, and we consciously used it to make choices that strengthened our love and friendship.

After we'd been married for awhile, the same ominous prophets of doom that had warned us how horrible life would get after marriage would step in and say, "Aha, but you just wait till the kids come along! Then life will hit you in the face, and you will be miserable like the rest of us. Then you'll see what marriage is *really* about." But, once again, I found this to be absolutely wrong. Things did change when our first child came along, and there were many challenges to adjust to, but as a challenge doubles, so does the opportunity for joy and fulfillment. We found that children in marriage became twice the work and twice the fun. We absolutely love being parents.

And wouldn't you know it, those same doomites are now approaching us saying things like, "Oh, well, you just wait till your kids are teenagers!" But we've stopped listening.

I'm not trying to imply that life gets easier with marriage and kids. It does get harder. But remember, it's *life* that's tough. The marriage is tested by the challenges of *life*, not the other way around. And even in those situations where it seems that the relationship is tough, when we look closely, it's usually our resistance to truth or our own selfishness that are making things tough.

If we are willing to be selfless, follow the gospel, and recognize that life is tough, with all it's bumps, bills, car troubles, and strained schedules, then we will see clearly that marriage *ROCKS!* It's the most fun, most fascinating journey of a lifetime, especially when it includes children. Marriage and family make up the greatest, happiest, and most fulfilling experiences of life.

Our Father in Heaven has declared that His main purpose—His dream, if you will, is to "bring to pass the immortality and eternal life" of His children (Moses 1:39). If the greatest Being in the universe finds His greatest hope, His greatest joy, and His greatest fulfillment in family, then what more can we aspire to than to work toward the same goal?

With His help, we can have that goal, and if we are faithful to the covenants we have made, it will last forever.

You Can Do It!

God wants your success even more than you do, though sometimes His promises take time. And what about those who, through no fault of their own, never have an opportunity to marry in this life?

Elder Richard G. Scott said:

> Some of you may feel lonely and unappreciated and cannot see how it will be possible for you to have the blessings of marriage and children or your own family. All things are possible to the Lord, and He keeps the promises He inspires His prophets to declare. Eternity is a long time. Have faith in those promises and live to be worthy

of them so that in His time the Lord can make them come true in your life. With certainty, you will receive every promised blessing for which you are worthy.[1]

President Ezra Taft Benson was even more direct when he promised:

> I also recognize that not all women in the Church will have an opportunity for marriage and motherhood in mortality. But if those of you in this situation are worthy and endure faithfully, you can be assured of all blessings from a kind and loving Heavenly Father—and I emphasize *all* blessings.
>
> I assure you that if you have to wait even until the next life to be blessed with a choice companion, God will surely compensate you. Time is numbered only to man. God has your eternal perspective in mind.[2]

Remember that your "singlehood" doesn't mean you're broken or lacking. It means you have something to work toward and look forward to. Every stage of life has goals built into it, and yours is one of the most fun, exciting, and rewarding.

You are God's child. He has given you the road to happiness. Whatever stage of dating you are in, love it. Enjoy the time you have. Enjoy the journey. Of course there will be times of frustration, loneliness, and deep heartache, but don't let your life be defined entirely by suffering. Find joy in what you are doing. Keep studying, keep pursuing goals, keep loving life. If you have a "bucket list," do the things you've always wanted to do. Your love and zest for life will make you more attractive and expose you to those who have similar hopes and dreams.

Remember above all else that God loves you. You are His child, and He will guide you through this wonderful stage of life. Talk to Him openly and regularly. Hang in there—you'll be surprised what God can do!

Marriage is ordained of God, and you will be guided as you seek this eternal blessing. You're diligent effort will act as a catalyst to your faith, and God will validate that faith by providing you with your deepest desires.

NOTES

1. Richard G. Scott, "The Eternal Blessings of Marriage," *Ensign*, May 2011, 94–97.
2. Ezra Taft Benson, "To the Single Adult Sisters of the Church," *Ensign*, Nov. 1988.

About the Author

Chas Hathaway is a musician, author, husband, dad, and ex-grave-digger. Throughout his life, Chas has enjoyed all types of creative writing. While serving a full-time mission in Johannesburg, South Africa, he also developed an unquenchable love of studying the gospel of Jesus Christ. After returning home, he earned an associates degree in music at Salt Lake Community College. While serving two years on LDS Institute Council, he experienced what he considers his greatest life accomplishment when he met and married Jenni Hair, who was also serving on the institute council. Now they are happily raising three beautiful, rambunctious children in Sanpete, Utah.